ID0606205

4. —

Invoking
Mary Magdalene

SIOBHÁN HOUSTON

Invoking
Mary Magdalene

ACCESSING THE WISDOM
of the DIVINE FEMININE

To Millie,

Many blessings!

Siobhán Houston

SOUNDS TRUE

Sounds True, Inc.
Boulder CO 80306

© 2006 Siobhán Houston ℗ Sounds True

SOUNDS TRUE is a trademark of Sounds True, Inc.
All rights reserved. No part of this book or CD may be used or reproduced
in any manner without written permission from the author and publisher.

Published 2006
Printed in Korea
Siobhán Houston:
        Invoking Mary Magdalene

ISBN 1-59179-422-6

Library of Congress Control Number 2005937139

12.5.2007 LA

I dedicate this book to my birth lineage of Jewish and Celtic women—especially my grandmothers, Lillian Bloom and Claire McLaughlin Houston; my mother, Dr. Gloria Bloom Houston; and my daughter, Gitavali Cornell. Most of all, I dedicate this book to my spouse, Rachel Miller—always the dream of my soul.

TABLE OF CONTENTS

Acknowledgments xi

Introduction 1

Chapter One 6
Who Is Mary Magdalene?

Chapter Two 12
Creating Sacred Space for the Magdalene Path

Chapter Three 22
Reveling in Bliss: Touching the Heart of the Beloved

Chapter Four 46
Embodying Compassion: Becoming a Vessel for Healing and Grace

Chapter Five 56
Opening to Wisdom: The Magdalene as Initiatrix into the Mysteries

Chapter Six 76
Accessing Power: Encountering the Magdalene as Dark Goddess

Chapter Seven 90
Continuing on the Magdalene Path

Notes 95

Additional Resources 99

About the Author 105

Acknowledgments

I WOULD LIKE to thank the contributors to this book, who generously permitted their prayers and rituals to be included—Ave Magdalena! Also, I offer my deepest appreciation to the friends, family, colleagues, and mentors who have graced my life—especially Allan Bloom, Mary Virginia Bunker, Dr. Daniel Fisher, Dr. Nicholas Goodrick-Clarke, Dr. Bruce Grelle, Mary Griffith, John Stuart Houston, Eleanor Palmer, Cynthia Reber-Maman, Randy Roark, Richard Smoley, Dr. Greg Tropea, Faith Weare, LeotaAnn Voll, Dr. Joel Zimbelman, and my late father, Donald Houston.

Introduction

USING THIS INTEGRATED book-and-CD as your guide and companion, I invite you to step onto the Magdalene Path. The Magdalene Path is a stream of spirituality in which Mary Magdalene is the principal figure, and all meditations, devotions, and rituals focus on her in one or more of her myriad aspects and forms. Though this particular path has been practiced in many forms for millennia, it must be re-imagined in every age. There are many entranceways to the Magdalene Path—*Invoking Mary Magdalene* is simply one among many. Indeed, you may have already embarked on this spiritual path and are now seeking direction and camaraderie in your quest.

Invoking Mary Magdalene is a complete set of experiences initiating you onto the Magdalene Path. By setting up an altar and working with these meditations, guided visualizations, and prayers, you invite direct and personal experience with the energies of the Magdalene. No previous knowledge of Mary Magdalene is assumed; both neophytes and advanced students will benefit greatly from incorporating these practices into their daily lives.

The Magdalene Path is a non-hierarchal, grassroots movement, inspired by a growing body of scholarship, literature, arts, and spirituality that honors the Divine Feminine. The Magdalene Path is self-defined, non-doctrinaire, and grounded in the experience of *gnosis,* or inner knowing. Those men and women who traverse this path answer the call of the Magdalene in countless ways—as solitary or group practitioners, authors, artists, dancers, healers, parents, priestesses and priests, teachers, and visionaries.

Mary Magdalene may be accessed by anyone regardless of ethnicity or religious tradition or background. Historically speaking, we know she was a Jewish woman and therefore is not only important to Christianity but to the Jewish tradition as well. Moreover, those devoted to the Goddess, as well as those who work within more esoteric systems like Kabbalah and Gnosticism, also have rightful claim to her.

Today, there is a groundswell of interest about the Magdalene, fueled by books such as *The DaVinci Code.* Dan Brown, author of *The DaVinci Code,* launched his thriller at a most opportune time—when the reading public was ready to encounter a new vision of Jesus and Magdalene. This book and others tapped into a deep hungering for knowledge about the feminine force that has been so long eclipsed in Western religion. It answers to a yearning arising from many quarters.

Authors, historians, psychologists, and filmmakers envision Mary Magdalene in a multiplicity of ways: as archetype, goddess, priestess, Tantric adept, saint, or some combination of these representations. Currently, men and women are partaking in Magdalene spirituality through churches, orders, and covens; by reading a channeled manuscript; or by enrolling in the many available workshops, tours, and retreats.

As I became aware of the great variety of contemporary Magdalene practices, I sensed an inner call for a book on this subject. Chatting with shopkeepers, baristas, and colleagues around Boulder, Colorado, affirmed my vision. Those I spoke with were intrigued by the many Magdalene groups and practices that my research unearthed, including James Twynan's experiments with the use of spikenard oil (said to be the "nard" with which Magdalene anointed Jesus), Tom Kenyon's channeling work, and Margaret Starbird's provocative historical excavations.

As the daughter of a Jewish mother and an Irish-American father, I have found Mary Magdalene to be of significant help in my own spiritual life, enabling me to skillfully traverse the liminal realm between Jewish and Catholic traditions. I have long been interested in the Magdalene's mysteries: how she weaves through the Jesus mythos and on through the Grail legends; the stories of her sailing to Glastonbury and to the South of France; and her possible connections with the Black Madonnas of Europe. Also, as the dark maiden of the *Song of Songs* and the beloved of Jesus, she figures prominently in my own contemplative and ritual practice, where she appears to me as a refraction of the Dark Mother who has also taken the forms of Kali (Hindu), Sekhmet (Egyptian), Hecate (classical Greek), and the Black Madonna (Christian), among others. The Dark Goddess shows herself to people in various ways, and one's relationship with any god or goddess is intensely personal and ultimately self-defined. Some devotees see her as an impersonal cosmic energy; some invoke her as a independent spiritual being in the form of a traditional goddess; and others call on her as an aspect of the self. It is possible, of course, to hold some or all these understandings simultaneously as one's experience with the Dark Goddess grows and changes.

When I ponder the Magdalene phenomenon, the concept of *kairos* comes to mind. Kairos is a Greek word, signifying the eternally full and present moment, the opportune time. Kairos (as opposed to *chronos* or linear time) denotes a moment when forces constellate to break through time as we perceive it, and something new appears. I believe that this new era of Magdalene consciousness promises to revolutionize Christianity and Western culture in ways we cannot yet conceive.

I look forward to being your guide as we make this journey together on the Magdalene Path. May the Holy Magdalene and her Companions, those in the visible and invisible worlds, illuminate our work together. There is a blessing on those who serve.

Siobhán Houston
Boulder, Colorado
October, 2005

CHAPTER
ONE

Who Is Mary Magdalene?

WHY ARE WE mesmerized by a woman who lived 2,000 years ago? And especially a woman who, until recently, was generally vilified as a prostitute, only of note because Jesus cleansed her of seven devils? Granted, this is not the only manner in which she appears in history and culture. In large part, she has been perceived through the ages as a redeemed woman turned disciple, someone who played a bit part in the drama of the Gospels, and a saint of fairly minor significance. Even though Mary Magdalene is mentioned more than any other woman in the New Testament, she has been accorded little importance in the mainstream Christian tradition.

A brief sketch of her life begins with her appearance in the Gospels as a Jewish woman from the Galilean town of Migdal. Most probably a single woman or widow of some wealth, she became a devoted follower of Jesus after he healed her of her affliction, described in the Bible as "seven demons." She traveled with Jesus and his disciples and helped support the fledgling movement financially. The Gospels place her as a witness to the crucifixion and burial of Jesus, and after the burial when she went to Jesus' resting place to dress his body, she discovered his empty tomb. Perhaps most importantly, the New Testament tells us that Mary Magdalene was the first to see the resurrected Jesus. She conveys this glorious news to his other disciples, thus earning herself the title "Apostle to the Apostles."

By the early Middle Ages, the Church conflated the stories of three different women mentioned in the New Testament and concluded that Mary Magdalene was a redeemed prostitute. Pope Gregory the Great made a formal pronouncement validating this view in 591 CE and it became official Catholic teaching, although it has no historical grounding. The Church rescinded this declaration in 1969, but Mary Magdalene's persona as a harlot turned faithful follower is still lodged in our collective consciousness. Despite this view, Magdalene emerged as the most popular saint during the Middle Ages, highly praised by the Church as a paragon and model of repentance. Traditional devotional practices to St. Mary Magdalene generally uphold the erroneous view of her as prostitute, and so I have chosen not to include them in this program. Instead, I draw on contemporary practices in which Mary Magdalene is imagined in more positive ways.

While Mary Magdalene's history as a religious and cultural icon is far too long to relate here, I want to call attention to one significant historical development. In the 1940s, a cache of ancient documents surfaced in the Egyptian desert, an event I discuss in Chapter Five. One result of this find is that some of the early Christian texts discovered mention Mary

Magdalene in revolutionary ways—as a teacher, a leader in the Christian community, and even as an incarnation of Wisdom.

As more primary documents of the early Christian era come to light, scholars are discovering that much of Magdalene's story seems to have been suppressed by rival factions in the early church. Little by little, the layers obscuring Mary Magdalene's role in the early Jesus movement are being worn away; new gospels are unearthed and new interpretations of Biblical texts emerge. Moreover, the public is learning of the countless ancient legends about Mary Magdalene, transmitted for the most part through the oral tradition in Europe. Wondrous tales of her marriage to Jesus, her mothering of a daughter, and her travels to Western Europe are now discussed openly, and many have an almost unquenchable desire to find out more about this enigmatic woman.

Admittedly, the reality of Mary Magdalene's earthly life will never be fully grasped but will always be slipping from us, concealed behind a shroud of myth, supposition, and mystery. For those who worship her as a form of the Goddess or an incarnation of the Gnostic wisdom-figure Sophia, for those who pray to her as a saint or who follow her channeled alchemical teachings, I suspect historical accuracy fades into the background.

As author Nicholas Whitehead noted in a 1997 interview, "I think that people respond to symbols and archetypal patterns, and if the Christ life is anything, it's an archetypal pattern. We need to remember that there's never one level on which you can interpret any kind of sacred history, because history is something that always expresses a certain point of view."[1]

For further exploration of the history of the Magdalene, I recommend the highly acclaimed *Mary Magdalene: Myth and Metaphor* by Susan Haskins. Jane Schaberg's book, *Resurrection Of Mary Magdalene: Legends, Apocrypha, and the*

Christian Testament, is also a fascinating read and provides a solid foundation for future studies.

Now that we have looked in brief at Mary Magdalene as a historical figure, we can proceed to the next chapter, which discusses how to construct a personal altar to the Magdalene as a prerequisite for the actual Magdalene Path practices. ✤

CHAPTER
TWO

Creating Sacred Space for the Magdalene Path

THE FIRST PHASE of the Magdalene Path is to construct an altar, a special place where you will go on a regular basis to relate to the Magdalene. Most people will find it advantageous to have a tangible, established site for meditation and reflection, even though making a personal altar to the Magdalene is not essential in order to walk her path. Since this is your personal shrine, you are free to include anything of meaning, whether or not it is traditionally considered religious or spiritual. This is a time to look at your spirituality with a fresh eye—to be playful, imaginative, resourceful, and perhaps irreverent. Perusing a book like *Altars and Icons* by Jean McCann*, which portrays the sacred personal spaces of a diverse group of individuals, is a great way to start this creative process.

* For more information on books, companies, and organizations mentioned in this book, please see the Additional Resources section on page 99.

An important caveat for all the practices in this book, including the suggestions in this chapter, is that you should choose those activities with which you resonate and that you can fit into your schedule without undo strain. These practices are offered as havens that allow you to *be* for a time, rather than *do*. Turning them into goal-oriented chores to somehow fit into your busy schedule is counterproductive. And since prayer and meditation are non-linear activities, their quality is not determined by the amount of time spent on them. Remember to treat yourself kindly.

A low table in the corner of a room, a shelf or bookcase, or even a windowsill is a perfectly acceptable site for your shrine. If your altar is set up in a room that you also use for other purposes (which is the case for most of us), there is a simple way to mark out your consecrated space: obtain a rug or mat specifically designated for use during your meditation time, and then fold or roll it up and stash it away when you are finished. The unfurled rug or mat denotes the area as a *temenos*—or sacred precinct—and temporarily differentiates it from the other activities taking place in the room. With regular use, the sublime energies generated by your practice will permeate your temenos, which will in turn assist you in entering a meditative state more quickly.

Your shrine may be adorned in a simple or elaborate way, depending on your personal tastes and the amount of time you wish to devote to it. For the most part, constructing a shrine starts with some favorite and evocative objects—such as pictures of special places and people, statues, natural items like stones and feathers, and other mementos—and then evolves organically as you add and take away objects over time. A candle and a Magdalene icon or print is a wonderful focal point, and that may be all you need or want for your altar, at least initially.

One way to start creating your altar is to ask yourself: what colors evoke the Magdalene for me? The altar clothes, stones, candles, and other decorative elements may then reflect these suggestive hues. For example, my current devotion to the Magdalene focuses on her Dark Goddess aspect, and so my altar to her is decorated in crimson, black, and gold, reflecting this orientation. It consists of a small, low table against a wall in my home office, adorned with a black and red embroidered cloth from India, red candles, and a little handmade ceramic bowl my daughter made to hold water, flowers, or other offerings. Several deities (sacred statues) crowd my tiny shrine space, including the Black Madonna of Notre Dame de Meymac, an imposing and vividly colorful Kali, and smaller deities of Kali and Shiva carved from soapstone. I also have a brass *ankh* (the Egyptian symbol of life), a piece of basalt (a rock associated with Sekhmet, a powerful Egyptian goddess), a photo of a French Magdalene statue, and stones from holy sites like Glastonbury, Cornwall, and Rennes-le-Chateau. My Magdalene altar is only one of a number of shrines—my spouse and I call our décor style "Little Altars Everywhere," since our home and garden teem with both formal and whimsical shrines, like the one composed of plastic wind-up animal toys.

Certain symbols are historically associated with Mary Magdalene, and you may wish to have these represented in your place of worship. She is often shown with a skull, an alabaster jar, a book, and a red egg. The skull most probably represents the transient nature of this earthly realm: the Magdalene may be gazing at it meditatively, as in Domemico Feti's painting "The Repentant Mary Magdalene," or the skull may be resting at her feet, as it does in the statue of her in the famous medieval French church of Rennes-le-Chateau. Another ubiquitous image is a book, either open or closed, which alludes to her role as guardian of the mysteries and of wisdom in general.

The alabaster jar recalls the scenes in the New Testament when a woman, usually assumed to be Magdalene, anoints Jesus with costly ointment from a vessel; it also suggests Mary Magdalene's larger mythic roles as priestess and healer. Finally, the red egg comes from a story told for hundreds of years in the Orthodox Christian tradition. According to this legend, Mary Magdalene related the incident of Jesus' resurrection to the dinner guests of the emperor Tiberius Caesar. Caesar ridiculed her, saying that a man could no more rise from the dead than the egg in her hand could turn red. The egg immediately turned crimson, and to this day red eggs are an important part of the Orthodox Christian holiday of *Pascha* (Easter).

Devotional statues or deities are integral elements of my own altars. I purchased most of these over the years from almost any spiritual tradition you might imagine, including reproductions of Sophia, the Gnostic Christ, Isis, Diana of Ephesus, Mary Magdalene, numerous Black Madonnas, and the four archangels—Gabriel, Uriel, Michael, and Raphael. The objects that you choose to include on your altar should also be a representative of the various aspects of your spiritual path as it unfolds for you.

PRAYER SHAWLS

A customary practice in many spiritual traditions is the use of a cloak, wrap, or mantle reserved for prayer and donned before commencing with meditation. The act of putting on special clothing signals to your subconscious that you are now entering a different state of consciousness, and, like entering your temenos, it facilitates a meditative state of mind. If the shawl is sizeable enough, such as a large Jewish *tallit* (also called a *tallis*), it may serve as a sort of tent to completely insulate you from the outside world and assist you with concentration. *Tallitot* may be bought at any Judaica or synagogue gift shop, often with a neckpiece embroidered with a Hebrew verse and made of wool, cotton, or silk. Other types of prayer shawls, such as *chadars* from India or the simple white silk Buddhist *kata,* have divine names printed in Sanskrit on them and are readily available at Indian and Tibetan gift shops.

Making your own prayer shawl can be an excellent meditative practice in itself. Organizations like the Shawl Ministry, founded in 1998 by Jane Bristow and Victoria Galo, have made conscious crafting popular in recent times. The Ministry's web site offers free shawl patterns to make for yourself or others, as well as prayers, intentions, rituals, photos, inspirational stories, and blessings to be said during the creation process. Tara Jon Manning's book *Mindful Knitting: Inviting Contemplative Practice to the Craft* has an easy pattern for a kata (a ceremonial Buddhist scarf), accompanied by insightful meditation instructions from the Tibetan Buddhist tradition.

Simple knitted, crocheted, quilted, or sewn shawls are easy to make—the Shawl Ministry site includes many suggestions, and you can also search the Internet for many other available free patterns. If you do not sew, a shawl may be fashioned from a piece of material you love—perhaps silk, cotton, or linen. Cut a piece of fabric wide enough to reach from wrist to wrist (or as wide as you wish)—if you use the full width of the fabric (usually 44"–45"), you will not need to hem the already-woven lengthwise edges (selvedges). Turn the unfinished edges under, making a hem about ½-inch wide. Secure the hem using the no-sew Stitch Witchery® or another fusible web product that bonds two layers of fabric together, and then iron the garment.

Whether you make or buy a shawl, you may choose to embellish it with symbols special to you or those associated with the Magdalene, using beads, feathers, iron-on or sewn appliqués, embroidery, or fabric paint. In her book *Magdalene's Lost Legacy,* Margaret Starbird contends that certain images were used in a secret emblematic language in late medieval Europe by "heretical" Christians whose tenets included belief in the marriage between Mary Magdalene and Jesus and a royal bloodline carried by their descendants. In Starbird's estimation, some of these emblems—concealed in artwork, tarot cards, and paper watermarks—included mermaids, unicorns, towers, castles (the Hebrew word *migdal* means tower), and the fleur-de-lis (a traditional floral design representing the three petals of an iris tied by an encircling band).

I once made a great shawl from a discarded silk shirt by cutting out the useable parts of the garment and cobbling them together to form a rectangular piece of material. Using colorful fabric markers, I then embossed it with poems and random phrases from my favorite mystic authors. Another of my meditation mantles came into being after I returned from my first trip to Glastonbury and experienced a strange, intense yearning to have as many bright green objects around me as possible. To pacify this urge, I crocheted a scintillating apple-green shawl in Lion Brand's Homespun®, a soft, silky, washable textured yarn available in a kaleidoscope of colors. Wrapped up in my vibrant shawl, I feel connected once again to the lush and verdant moors around Glastonbury, even as I meditate in my home in the foothills of the Rocky Mountains.

Before using your shawl, bring it to your altar and dedicate it with an intention such as, "May the wearing of this shawl help me attain the clarity and compassion of the Magdalene," or "May the Weaver who wove this world bless me as I pray."

PRAYER BEADS

Prayer beads are another optional accoutrement on the Magdalene Path. Whether counting Sanskrit mantra repetitions or tallying Hail Marys with a traditional rosary, the very concrete act of sliding beads through your fingers is known to help ground and focus your prayer. In their myriad forms as ropes of beads or knotted cords, prayer beads are variously called rosaries, *chtokis* (Russia), *japa-malas* (India, Tibet, Nepal), *tasbih* (Persia), and *komboloi* (Greece), among other terms. Even within the realm of Christian rosaries, great variety exists, including chaplets, psalters, Bridget rosaries, and Anglican rosaries.

Over the millennia, devotees have used innumerable types of materials for their prayer beads, including semi-precious and common stones, gemstones and pearls, crystals, seeds, wood, shells, clay, and even crushed rose petals formed into pellets (the source of the word "rosary"). Because the symbol of a skull is so intricately connected to Mary Magdalene, bone prayer beads (usually made from water-buffalo bone and often carved in the shape of small skulls) are especially appropriate in Magdalene devotions. Used primarily by devotees of the Hindu goddess Kali, bone *malas* may be bought in Indian and Tibetan shops.

Over the years, I have collected and made several sets of beads, my favorite being an Anglican rosary of jasper stones purchased from the Solitaries of DeKoven, a religious community in Santa Anna, Texas. Using this 33-bead circlet, I feel a heart connection with the unknown hermit who crafted my rosary, as if he or she was my companion in the act of contemplation. If you would like to learn more about the history and symbology of prayer beads as well as instructions for making different kinds, I recommend the book *A String and a Prayer: Making and Using Prayer Beads* by Eleanor Wiley and Maggie Oman Shannon.

MARY MAGDALENE GARDENS

The association and cultivation of flowers and plants in honor of the Virgin Mary and other Biblical figures is an enchanting and little-known practice coming down to us from the Middle Ages. Specific flowers and plants—some of whose religious names are rosary vine (Heart Vine), Trinity (Shamrock), Star of Bethlehem, Mother-of-Thousands (Spanish Moss), Herb of Grace (Rue), and Our Lady's Mantle (Lady's Mantle)—were associated with Biblical characters and the holy virtues in medieval and Renaissance popular culture. Drawing on this familiar botanical language, medieval churches often featured stone carvings of flowers and plants as mnemonic devices designed to enhance the faith of parishioners. These practices—which fell to the wayside over the centuries due in part to the Protestant Reformation—have revived in the last century, with many parishes and individuals sowing devotional gardens for meditation and prayer.

Since many Christian customs, holidays, and worship sites overlaid and co-opted pre-existing pagan conventions, it is not surprising that a number of these botanicals were held sacred to a panoply of pagan divinities. For example, Harold N. Moldenke writes in *Horticulture* magazine:

> *Ivy was a plant dedicated to Bacchus; the holly and the Yule log were associated with early Druid rites, yet all three soon were used in Christian festivals in England. Plants that had hitherto been sacred to or dedicated to Venus, or to her Scandinavian counterpart, Freya, or to some other great female divinity, now became associated with Mary, mother of Jesus ... The plant known in old Iceland as "Freyje's Heir" became Our Lady's Hair, and "Maria's fern" in England now is known as maidenhair. Its scientific name, Adiantum capillus-veneris, indicates that in more ancient times it was dedicated to Venus.[2]*

Growing an indoor garden dedicated to the Magdalene unites you with the natural world even within your indoor meditation space. It recalls the luxuriant, sensual nature imagery of the biblical *Song of Songs*, long associated with Mary Magdalene and traditionally read on her feast day in the Roman Catholic church (July 22nd): "I am the Rose of Sharon, the Lily of the Valley ... "

Begin by choosing a decorative planter dish or glass terrarium, and then pick out appropriate plants given the light levels and climate of your meditation space. A statuette of Mary Magdalene or a laminated picture of her placed amidst the plants is a lovely addition to your little plot. An amazing resource to consult as you plan your devotional garden is the Mary Gardens web site, which features extensive lists of plants and their symbolic associations, along with complete gardening instructions for both indoor and outdoor gardens, fascinating historical facts, mail-order nursery information, prayers and blessings, and photos and descriptions of contemporary gardens.

The ways in which you choose to create a meditation space will grow over time, but I would suggest that you at least set up an altar before you go further. Once you have established your altar, you can continue with Chapter Three, which begins instruction in the actual practices of invoking Mary Magdalene. These practices are instrumental in establishing and deepening your devotional relationship to her. ✤

CHAPTER
THREE

Reveling in Bliss:
Touching the Heart of the Beloved

IN WESTERN RELIGION, the expression "the love of God" is a commonly used phrase, generally understood as paying homage to God in an attitude of awe and reverence and worshipping the Divine from afar. The idea of loving God, though, takes on a much more intimate cast—that of communing with one's Beloved—in some Eastern forms of spirituality as well as in many of the Western inner and contemplative traditions. Sufi devotional poetry, for example, is studded with allusions to God as "the Friend" or "Beloved." This ecstatic form of poetry describes a euphoric, wild, drunken adoration of the Divine, a passionate, unbridled love that eclipses all earthly concerns and societal conventions.

It was not uncommon for medieval Catholic nuns to take Jesus as their spouse: this custom is called "theogamy" or marriage to a god.[3] Gertrude the Great, a notable woman mystic of the 13th century, saw herself as married to Jesus: "At the age of twenty-five, she experienced a religious conversion in the form of the Lord Jesus, who appeared to her as a beautiful young man and invited her into close union with him. Gertrude's mysticism is always in this spousal form."[4] Several centuries later, the Renaissance philosopher Giordano Bruno (c. 1548–1600) spoke of his relationship to Sophia (Wisdom) in conjugal terms: "The divine Sophia I have loved and sought since my youth; I have desired her to be my spouse. Ever have I loved her beautiful, radiant form."[5]

In medieval India, the Hindu Vaishnava system of *bhakti-yoga* (devotional yoga) developed highly sophisticated categories of relationship (*rasa*) to God, including *santa* (awe and reverence), *vatsalya* (parental attitude toward God), *dasya* (servant of God), *sakhya* (being friends and playmates with God), and *madhurya* (passionate, romantic love). Underlying this conception is the view that God's highest aspect is that of the divine person, who delights in close relationship with God's creation, as opposed to being only an impersonal spiritual force or presence. According to this theology, madhurya or conjugal love is considered to be the most rarefied relationship with the Holy. Human romantic love, as splendid and gratifying as it may be, is seen as a faint reflection of a blissful relationship to God, the original lover of the soul.

The path of devotion is founded on the idea that elevated spiritual beings exist on some level, however we conceive of them, and therefore so does the possibility for a close and loving relationship between a human and his or her Beloved. On the Magdalene Path, then, to whom are we referring when we speak of the Beloved? We may be speaking of Jesus, Mary Magdalene, Jesus and Magdalene together, or the Goddess Sophia (Wisdom), to name a few possibilities. Given that there is an endless array of ways to approach the Divine, how do you choose which aspect to venerate? Perhaps the best advice is to observe which spiritual being resonates most strongly with you. Who conjures up in you deep feelings of devotion? This may very well change over time, and the form of the Holy that you relate to this week or this year may shift with the next.

One possible method is to envision Jesus (or Yeshua, Jesus' name in ancient Aramaic) and Mary Magdalene, bound to each other in a multi-faceted relationship, as the Beloved Ones. This model of Jesus and Magdalene echoes other divine couplings such as Radha-Krishna or Shiva-Shakti of the Hindu tradition, and Yahweh-Shekhinah in mystical Judaism, all examples of eternally paired male and female god-aspects whose liaison creates and permeates the universe. A number of early Gnostic Christian theologians believed that Jesus, as Christ the Logos (Divine Order or Word), and Magdalene, as Christ the Sophia (Wisdom), together form the Christos, the Anointed One.

On another level, seeing Jesus and Magdalene as a married couple within their community, which many believe to be historical fact, adds a human element to the mythological dimensions illustrated previously. In *The Goddess in the Gospels*, Margaret Starbird speaks of the return of Mary Magdalene as "restoring the historical wife of Jesus to her rightful place at his side and at the same time, on a deeper plane, thinking of how that will help to restore the 'partnership paradigm'—the imaging of the Divine as both Bride and Bridegroom—in the holy inner sanctum of our collective psyche."[6] The idea of Jesus and Magdalene as a wedded or otherwise romantically involved couple—whether their liaison is seen as human, spiritual, archetypal, or some combination of these three attributes—offers a relationship model that is affirming and inspiring to many, one in which both parties are enlightened, powerful, and independent. This model may also inform a more inclusive Christianity, one in which the Divine Feminine in all its strength and beauty is embraced as integral to theology, spiritual practice, and institutional organization.

Drawing on another primeval tradition, that of the *hieros gamous* (Greek for sacred marriage), may further enrich our understanding of Mary Magdalene's possible relationship to Jesus. Ancient Mediterranean civilizations such as Mesopotamia and Sumeria celebrated these sacred marriage ceremonies millennia before the advent of Christianity. In the hieros gamous ceremony, a woman, perhaps a priestess, assumed the role of a powerful goddess (such as Inanna or Ishtar), and a man, possibly a high-ranking ruler, took on the identity of a god (like Dumuzi or Tammuz). Amid various elaborate procedures, the couple joined sexually; whether this happened symbolically or in fact is debated, as is the ritual's ultimate purpose. Some theorize that by this sexually charged act, the king was chosen as a consort of the goddess and was anointed by her and empowered to rule. Others believe its purpose was to increase the land's fruitfulness through the enactment of a fertility rite between the two divine representatives. Some modern Biblical interpreters point to Magdalene's anointing of Jesus with costly ointment as a "king-making" gesture along the lines of the hieros gamous, suggesting that she was a priestess of Isis or Astarte choosing her consort. I will discuss this in greater detail in the next chapter, within the context of Magdalene as healer.

In addition to venerating Jesus and Magdalene together, we may also relate to Magdalene *alone* as the Beloved Holy One. In this aspect she is seen as independent of Yeshua, whole unto herself, and beyond characterizations as Bride or Mother. It may seem radical to imagine Mary Magdalene as an all-powerful goddess and even more far-reaching to relate to her as a sister, friend, or lover. But if each refraction or incarnation of the Divine possesses all the qualities of the Divine, then it follows that Magdalene herself may be worshipped as the fully Divine. While Hindu theology often depicts the goddess Shakti (sometimes called Kali) accompanied by her eternal consort Shiva, frequently she is worshipped alone, as the omnipotent One.

Thus, devotees of either gender may approach the Goddess in her form as Mary Magdalene in a servant mood, a mood of friendship or sisterhood, or even in an amorous fashion. Reading selections from the Gnostic texts will acquaint you with fresh and powerful portrayals of Magdalene that stand out in stark contrast to the insipid images of her as penitential prostitute, which circulated for centuries by the Church. Works like the *Dialogue of the Savior,* the *Gospel of Mary Magdalene,* and the *Gospel of Thomas* describe her enlightened state of being, her high standing in the Christian community, and her authoritative teaching role, among other qualities.

Whatever divine form you choose to adore, there are all sorts of methods to help you heighten your attachment to the Beloved. A particularly potent means is to quietly recite divine names or mantras repeatedly, so the Beloved's name becomes "engraved on the heart." You may also recite the holy names in your mind, while waiting on queue at the bank, riding the bus, or doing any variety of daily tasks. Another approach is to chant, sing, and even dance in praise to the Holy, either alone in front of your altar or with others. While praying alone is excellent, jubilant congregational chanting and worship can be an intense and singular experience that magnifies the individual's prayer many times over. As the Mary Magdalene movement grows and matures, I hope the opportunities to pray in fellowship with others increases—already this is happening on a small scale, with people convening to celebrate Mary Magdalene's feast day in new and wonderful ways.

Another long-established manner to increase love for the Holy consists of making regular offerings of water, fruit, flowers, and incense at your altar. Hindu deity worship has developed this activity to a high form: deities are dressed daily in sumptuous silk clothes, fresh flower garlands, and jewels; offered gastronomic delicacies several times a day; and provided small beds in which to sleep—all of which are meant to fan the flames of devotion as well as an attitude of intimate service to God. Such opulence, while impressive, is not necessary—a simple offering of an incense stick or a single flower is at least as valuable if offered in a spirit of genuine devotion.

Prayers to Mary Magdalene

An essential form of devotion is prayer, and this chapter offers a number of different prayers to the Magdalene. The first prayer takes the form of a simple self-dedication in which you introduce yourself to the Magdalene, state your intention to traverse the Magdalene Path, and ask for her blessings. Following this consecration is a *novena* (Latin for "nine"), a private or public prayer that is said each day on nine consecutive days, often those preceding a saint's feast day. For example, a traditional Magdalene novena would begin on July 14 and would finish on Mary Magdalene's July 22 feast day. Novenas are an ancient Christian practice whose beginnings are unclear; originally they may have been Roman pagan forms of supplication.

Also included in this chapter is a traditional Anglican prayer to St. Mary Magdalene followed by a set of seven prayers written by a contemporary Magdalene devotee. The practices in this chapter conclude with a ritual for Mary Magdalene's feast day. Magdalene's feast day has been celebrated for at least twelve hundred years, and we know this because the 8th-century English monk Bede mentions its observation in his writings. While celebrating this ritual on July 22 is very special, it may be performed at any time during the year. Although it was written for a group, it may be adapted for a solitary practitioner.

Meditation Position

In the Western mysteries, the recommended meditation posture is sitting upright in a straight-backed chair with feet flat on the ground or resting on a footstool. While some teachers in the Western inner traditions explicitly discourage their students from sitting on the floor, my advice is to sit whichever way is most comfortable for you. I prefer to be seated on the floor in a cross-legged position supported by a *zafu* (a traditional Zen cushion filled with buckwheat husks). Depending on whether you sit on the floor or in a chair should determine the height of your altar, since you want to be eye level with it if possible. Keeping your body motionless is not necessary in this type of meditation; aim to be attentive to your body, rather than to disassociate from it.

Self-Dedication Prayer to the Magdalene Path

Light a candle and sit quietly before your altar for a few minutes, meditating on the Magdalene as you understand her. Then say these words: "Holy Magdalene, I have long heard your call. I now wish to dedicate myself to your path. Grace me with your compassion and initiate me into your mysteries, for my benefit and for the enlightenment of all living beings. So be it."

NOVENA TO MARY MAGDALENE [7]

Day One

Reading

I was sent forth from the power, and I have come
  to those who reflect upon me,
and I have been found among those who seek after me.
Thunder, Perfect Mind [8]

Reflection

Mary Magdalene, you who are the embodiment of the Holy Sophia, you have made yourself known once again in our world. You are indeed a full manifestation of the Holy One. Let us remember your great power and majesty even as we meditate on your human form.

Contemplation

The maidens saw her and called her happy;
the queens and concubines also, and they praised her.
Who is this that looks forth like the dawn,
Fair as the moon, bright as the sun,
Terrible as an army with banners?
Song of Solomon 6:9–10 [9]

Day Two

Reading

The Saviour loved Mary Magdalene more than all disciples. And he kissed her often on her mouth. The rest of the disciples were jealous of her. They asked and said to him: "Why do you love her more than all of us?" The Saviour answered and said to them, "Why do I not love you like her?"
Gospel of Phillip [10]

Reflection

From time immemorial, you as Christ the Sophia have been the consort of Christ the Logos. In your divine play as Yeshua's companion, you call us to integrate our internal female and male energies. Let us aspire to be as beloved to you as you are to Yeshua.

Contemplation

How fair and pleasant you are,
O loved one, delectable maiden!
Song of Solomon 7:6

Day Three

Reading

Then turning toward the woman, Jesus said to Simon, "Do you see this woman? I entered your house; you gave me no water for my feet, but she has bathed my feet with her tears and dried them with her hair. You gave me no kiss, but from the time I came in she has not stopped kissing my feet. You did not anoint my head with oil, but she has anointed my feet with ointment."
Gospel of Luke 7:44–46

Reflection

Washing the feet of another is a sign of humility and service, and this you offered to Yeshua, even though you are his equal in all respects. Let the purifying and sanctifying energies of your presence flow into our lives, through tears, through surging rivers, through refreshing fountains, and through the sea, rising and falling with the moon.

Contemplation

[You are] a garden fountain, a well of living water,
and flowing streams from Lebanon.
Song of Solomon 4:15

Day Four

Reading

Soon afterwards he went on through cities and villages, proclaiming and bringing the good news of the kingdom of God. The twelve were with him, as well as some women who had been cured of evil spirits and infirmities. Mary, called Magdalene, from whom seven demons had gone out ...
Gospel of Luke 8:1–2

Reflection

O Magdalene, you were healed and perfected through the cleansing of your seven subtle power centers (chakras). May we also release the seven veils of illusion concealing the brilliant clarity and bliss of our natural state of being.

Contemplation

Glory to Mary, because she has listened to her master, [she has] carried out his instructions with joy in her whole heart.

[Glory and] triumph to the soul of blessed Mary.
Manichaean Psalms [11]

Day Five

Reading

While he was at Bethany, in the house of Simon the leper, as he sat at the table, a woman came in with an alabaster jar of very costly ointment of nard, and she broke open the jar and poured the ointment on his head … Jesus said, " … [S]he has anointed my body beforehand for its burial. Truly I tell you, wherever the good news is proclaimed in the whole world, what she has done will be told in remembrance of her."
Gospel of Mark 14:3–9

Reflection

For millennia, priestesses and priests have used essential oils, such as myrrh, frankincense, and spikenard, to heal, transform, and initiate. By christening Yeshua in this way, you sealed him to you as your consort, O Queen of Heaven. May we go forth as healers and sages in your name to assist the reemergence of the Divine Feminine in our world.

Contemplation

While the king was on his couch,
my nard gave forth its fragrance.
Song of Solomon 1:12

Day Six

Reading

But Mary stood weeping outside the tomb. As she wept, she bent over to look into the tomb; and she saw two angels in white sitting where the body of Jesus had been lying, one at the head and the other at the feet.

They said to her, "Woman, why are you weeping?"

She said to them,

"They have taken away my Lord and I do not know where they have laid him."
Gospel of John 20:11–13

Reflection

When you discovered Yeshua's body had disappeared, you plunged into deep feelings of divine separation. Although we are forever united to you, Mary-Sophia, our confused perceptions trick us into thinking that we are somehow separate and alone. By meditating on your life, Magdalene, may we remember our true standing as empowered beings and co-creators of this world.

Contemplation

Upon my bed at night I sought him who my soul loves;
I sought him, but found him not;
I called him, but he gave no answer.
"I will rise now and go about the city,
in the streets and in the squares;
I will seek him whom my soul loves."
I sought him, but found him not.
Song of Solomon 3:1–2

Day Seven

Reading

Mary stood up, greeted them all, and said to her brothers, "Do not weep or grieve or be in doubt, for his grace will be with you all and will protect you. Rather let us praise his greatness, for he has prepared us and made us truly human."

Gospel of Mary [12]

Reflection

In death, our loved ones step over to another reality that we cannot readily perceive. By emulating your courage and insight, Magdalene, may we overcome obstacles and chimeras created by the mind and apprehend the world's true nature.

Contemplation

[F]or love is strong as death, passion fierce as the grave.
Its flashes are flashes of fire, a raging flame.
Many waters cannot quench love, neither can floods drown it.

Song of Solomon 8:6–7

Day Eight

Reading

Peter said to Mary: " … Tell us whatever you remember of any words he told you which we have not yet heard." Mary said to them: I will now speak to you of that which has not been given to you to hear."

Gospel of Mary [13]

Reflection

Yeshua transmitted secret teachings to you that were withheld from the other apostles. As we become more fully present to Reality, Magdalene, initiate us into the hidden wisdom you alone hold.

Contemplation

Jesus said, "It is to those [who are worthy of my] mysteries that I tell my mysteries."

Gospel of Thomas [14]

Day Nine

Reading

Mary said to them: "I will now speak to you of that which has not been given to you to hear. I had a vision of the Teacher, and I said to him: 'Lord I see you now in this vision.' And he answered, 'You are blessed, for the sight of me does not disturb you. There where is the nous, lies the treasure.'"

Gospel of Mary [15]

Reflection

Through means of the nous ("divine intelligence"), you apprehended the Teacher Yeshua in his new state of being, without alarm or unease. May our nous, our inner sight and luminous intelligence, be activated and amplified so we may envision the Real.

Contemplation

I am a lamp to you who see me.
Amen.
I am a mirror to you who perceive me.
Amen.
I am a door to you who knock on me.
Amen.
I am a way to you, you passerby.
Amen.

The Round Dance of the Cross [16]

SEVEN PRAYERS TO MARY MAGDALENE [17]

By Soror Lucia

I. Our Lady Magdalene

Our Lady Magdalene, holy and complete,

your mysteries are many,

Apostle of the Apostles,

blessed among women,

kindle in me the spark of wisdom

which guides from darkness into light.

2. Prayer for Gnosis

Glory is in the One,

and in the Logos

and in the Holy Sophia.

As I go forth in faith,

let glory be revealed.

3. The Mystery of Love

Love is the key to unlock the secrets

of compassion, empathy, and life.

I live to transcend this mortal coil

through the power of perfect love.

4. The Mystery of Faithfulness

For so long as the truth burns
in my secret heart of hearts,
may I walk the path of faithfulness
toward the limitless light.

5. The Mystery of Vision

From the past, let me learn,
for the present, let me live,
and for the future, let me strive.
May today be the holy benefactor of tomorrow.

6. The Mystery of the Circle of Life

Black, white, and red.
The egg, the phoenix, and the ouroborous.
May all things die, be transformed,
and live again in magnificence.

7. The Mystery of Seven

I shed the seven one by one,
through the miracle of the Logos,
and ascend to a realm beyond,
pure, transmutated, and free.

TRADITIONAL ANGLICAN PRAYER TO ST. MARY MAGDALENE

Grant unto us, most Merciful Father, that like as blessed Mary Magdalene
By loving thy Only-Begotten One above all things,
Obtained pardon of all her sins,
So she may secure for us everlasting blessedness
In [T]hy compassionate presence. [18]

FEAST DAY OF MARY MAGDALENE RITUAL (JULY 22ND)

By Lotus Moonwise [19]

(Note: Although the following is designed to be performed by a group, it may easily be adapted for a solitary practitioner. The ritual's power is not contingent on obtaining all the specified tools. If you do not have access to all the supplies, you can improvise by using alternate objects or your imagination.)

Tools

Red cloth to cover altar
Red candles (at least three, but more if desired)
Chalice with red wine (to symbolize the blood of Christ)
Alabaster jar (or other container), filled with a mixture of water and sea salt
Statue of Mary
Statue of Jesus
Dark-colored scarf or veil
Small crown of dried red roses for the statue of Mary
Plate with small pieces of bread
A cross

Spread the red cloth to cover your altar space. Place the dark veil over the statue of Mary and set this statue beside the statue of Christ. Have all other items laid out on the altar nearby.

Begin Ritual

1. *Purify your ritual space by sprinkling it with a mixture of water and sea salt.*

2. *Cast circle.*

"We create here sacred space, a temple between the worlds, a refuge where we can connect to the Divine Spirit within and invite the Divine Spirit of the universe to join with us. Join with us now in this space. So mote it be."

3. *Call quarters.*

"Hail to the Watchtowers of the East, Spirits of Air, Powers of the Mind, we invite you to this circle. May you bless us with clear thoughts. Come in peace and blessed be.

"Hail to the Watchtowers of the South, Spirits of Fire, Powers of the Soul, we invite you to this circle. May you bless us with heartfelt passion. Come in peace and blessed be.

"Hail to the Watchtowers of the West, Spirits of Water, Powers of Heart, we invite you to this circle. May you bless us with emotional empathy. Come in peace and blessed be.

"Hail to the Watchtowers of the North, Spirits of Earth, Powers of the Body, we invite you to this circle. May you bless us with physical health. Come in peace and blessed be."

4. *Set your intention.*

"We are present here this day to honor the Spirit of Mary Magdalene, to witness her re-union with her lost bridegroom and to restore her to her rightful place: as Mother, Lover, and Wife to the God. We come to honor her as a goddess in her own right, the other half of the dual nature of the Divine. Long has the Goddess been cast aside and forgotten. Now is the time for her re-emergence. We are spiritual midwives, acting as vessels for the Goddess. We are her Sacred Daughters. We are the soul of All That Is, in the flesh. It is time to remember her in her true form, not as sinful prostitute, but as the sacred, honored, and loved wife/sister/mother she is."

5. *The invocation to Mary.*

"In your three aspects—Mother, Sister, Wife—you are a symbol of the Triple Goddess. We light these three red candles now, to invite your energy, passion, and creative life force into this circle.

"Mary, called 'She Who Knows All,' you are all women: the passionate lover, the devoted wife, the independent maiden, equal partner, the teacher, and the student. Long have you been separated from your bridegroom, your chosen mate, your son and husband. You are she who knows the mystery of birth and death. You are she who has died and been reborn. You are she who has gnosis. You are she who acted as counsel and most cherished partner to the Christ. It is time for you to come out of hiding, to remove the shame and secrecy that has shrouded the truth about your identity."

Remove the dark veil from the Mary statue.

"Mary, you are free to shine and radiate your truth and beauty, joy and love onto the world. The veil has been lifted and your heart is free. You stand side by side with your lover and husband. We place you now in your rightful place, as Queen of Heaven and Earth."

Put red rose crown on the head of the Mary statue.

"May we always remember you and honor you. May we walk in beauty and know that you are with us, guiding us and loving us. May the example of your love with the Christ guide us in our lives as well. For with him, you

are your own being, your own woman. You are one with him in true uncondi-
tional love. The kind of love that demands nothing of sacrifice. The kind of
love that is freely given. The kind of love that expands the universe. The pure
spark of creative union that continues the cycle of evolution and creation.
You represent the Sacred Feminine in me, just as your chosen King, Jesus, represents the Divine Masculine within. Together, you both represent the perfect
balance of these energies in my own soul. We are sparks of you both."

6. *Enact the symbolic re-union.*

"As you stand side by side, once again the two halves are together, just as
they were in the beginning. There is such beauty and completeness in your
union, and it is a symbol for the renewal of life. The cross and the cauldron
are two sides of the same coin. The God is carried within the Goddess. The
blood of his body is contained within this chalice, this holy grail. This blood
lives on. It is renewed through her body, the vessel of all life. Within each of
us is the Christ Seed, the gnosis, the consciousness of our Divine Selves and
our connection to All That Is."

*Each person in the group will now dip a piece of bread into the wine and take a bite. Each
person repeats these words:*

"I honor the union of both within me, as I honor the integration of my
god self and my goddess self. I am All That Is. I am She Who Knows All."

7. *Thank Goddess and God.*

"We thank you, Mary and Jesus, for being here with us today in this sacred
space. May the joy of your union live on in our hearts. May the inspiration
you have given us and the love we have felt here continue on in our everyday
lives. May we remember always that you are with us and we are never alone.
Thank you for all your blessings."

8. *Thank and release the four quarters.*

"Watchtowers of North, Spirits of Earth, thank you for joining with us in this circle and lending your energies here. Hail and farewell. Go in peace and blessed be.

"Watchtowers of West, Spirits of Water, thank you for joining with us in this circle and lending your energies here. Hail and farewell. Go in peace and blessed be.

"Watchtowers of South, Spirits of Soul, thank you for joining with us in this circle and lending your energies here. Hail and farewell. Go in peace and blessed be.

"Watchtowers of East, Spirits of Air, thank you for joining with us in this circle and lending your energies here. Hail and farewell. Go in peace and blessed be."

9. *Open the circle.*

"May this circle now be open, yet never broken. Merry meet, merry part, and merry meet again."

By making use of these practices, you are now formally vowed to the Magdalene Path. You have linked yourself to Mary Magdalene through intensive prayer and the performance of the feast day ritual. This ceremony will further crystallize your connection with Mary Magdalene through the powerful effects of symbolic reenactment. The next chapter highlights the Magdalene's importance as a healer as well as techniques to enhance compassion and renewal, both for yourself and others. ✣

CHAPTER
FOUR

Embodying Compassion:
Becoming a Vessel for Healing and Grace

MARY MAGDALENE IS revealed in legend, art, and text as both healed
and healer. One of her most well-known appearances in the New Testament
is when Jesus miraculously purges seven demons from her (Luke 8:1–3).
Following this exorcism, she joins Jesus' band of followers, contributes financially to his mission, and eventually becomes his closest disciple, at least
according to some early texts. By the Middle Ages, Magdalene was the most
popular saint in Europe, known as variously as the apostle to the apostles,
a former prostitute cleansed of sin, and a healer—and she often appears in
works of art holding a jar of balm to denote this last role.

We should note that although the Gospels mention her seven times
(more than any other woman), she is never connected with prostitution or

adultery. Even so, by the 6th century Christianity transformed Magdalene into a former "woman of the night," conflating her with two other New Testament characters. Not surprisingly, Jesus' exorcism of Magdalene has customarily been interpreted as Mary Magdalene being freed from her heinous sins and rank desires. Other ways of looking at this event, however, include a physical or mental healing at the hands of Jesus, or that his actions constituted a clearing of her seven major chakras or energy centers. By this deed, some suggest, the Magdalene became fully initiated, a transparent channel for spiritual knowledge, and the preeminent disciple of Jesus. In the next chapter, we will explore her healing further, interpreting the event through the Gnostic theology of seven universal levels or planes.

As mentioned previously, Mary Magdalene is usually shown with specific accoutrements, several of which symbolize her role as wise woman and healer. The skull, one of her ubiquitous emblems, is a potent image for healing, as is the cup or chalice that she sometimes bears, as on the cover of this book. The shape and function of both cups and skulls call to mind the cauldron and the alembic (the glass container used by alchemists), both vessels in which transformation and metamorphosis occur.

The cup also carries the rich symbolism of sustenance, holy blood, and healing waters, all intimately connected with goddess energies. "Goddess shrines are nearly always found near wells, springs, lakes, or the sea. In Christian times, churches, hermitages, and anchorages—especially those dedicated to women saints—were to be found near a sacred well or spring."[20] Additionally, the skull reminds us that all of our human bodies will come to rest in the earth someday, bringing a leveling and compassionate quality to our interactions with others, along with an awareness of the world as transitory.

"The Myrrh-Bearer"—an epithet for the Magdalene used in the Orthodox Christian tradition—further points to her role as healer. This evocative title alludes to her visit to Yeshua's tomb to anoint his body with spices. Myrrh is a sweet-smelling resin (dried tree sap) and was one of the most commonly used oils in the ancient Middle East and Mediterranean. It was traditionally employed as an ingredient in incense and perfumes and was used to embalm and fumigate.

A position that is analogous to healer is that of "priestess," one of Magdalene's various guises. Numerous contemporary writers, like Margaret Starbird and Clystra Kinstler, propose that Mary Magdalene may have been an acolyte and initiate of one of the many powerful goddess religions of the time, such as the cults of Isis and Inanna. Goddess worship was not limited to gentiles, and although it is little known, ancient Jews worshipped fertility goddesses, primarily Asherah. Her statues were venerated in the Jerusalem temple until competing Jewish factions prevailed and stamped out that practice. In their intriguing book *The Magdalen Manuscript*, Tom Kenyon and Judi Sion suggest that not only was Mary Magdalene a highly ranked priestess of Isis, but she was also skilled in Egyptian meditation practices and sexual magic, the secrets of which she shared with Jesus in order to strengthen his etheric (subtle) body.

In popular folk traditions in France, Mary Magdalene is closely linked with healing due to her association with the Black Madonnas or Black Virgins. These medieval dark-colored stone or wood statues depict a Madonna and Child, who are believed by many to be Christianized figures of the Egyptian goddess Isis and her son Horus. Why legends persistently connect the Magdalene to the Black Madonnas, especially those in France, will be explored in greater depth in Chapter Five. Since the Black Madonnas are intrinsically connected with miraculous healing phenomenon, however, it is appropriate to bring them into this discussion.

The many hundreds of Black Madonnas (three hundred in France alone) are primarily situated in European Catholic churches and have been coupled with miracle working since the Middle Ages. For example, in the nave of an ancient Roman Catholic chapel deep in the heart of Bavaria, the Black Madonna known as "Our Lady of Altötting" presides over her pilgrims as she has for centuries in her church known as the "Lourdes of Germany." Our Lady of Altötting's many supplicants have left crutches, canes, and other indications of their curative experiences at the shrine of this medieval Black Madonna. One legend of her powers says that, in 1489, a child who had drowned came back to life after being brought to her altar, and this is only one of the many miracles credited to her.

Crossing Europe west to Spain, the city of Montserrat is the site for one of the most famous Black Madonnas. *La Morenata* ("the little black one") is known throughout the country for its amazing curative powers and miraculous occurrences attributed to her intercession. Currently over one million pilgrims visit her every year, many of them women petitioning for blessings of fertility.

Given that one of Magdalene's central aspects is that of healer and intercessor for the ill, dispossessed, and marginalized of this world, how may of us on the Magdalene Path embody and radiate her qualities of compassion and caring? Self-compassion must be our starting place—and that necessitates a stepping away from our "monkey mind," whose critical voice runs endlessly inside our heads. Simultaneously, we need to accept our birthright not only to ask for blessings but also to transmit blessings to others. Since we are each a holy being, we have the capacity and moreover the duty to do this, by prayer, thoughts, and actions. Interestingly, Dante Gabriel Rossetti's painting on the book's cover, "The Damsel of the Sanc Grael," shows the Grail Maiden holding up her right hand in the sign of benediction. Energy streams forth from our hands, even if unseen by us, and the hands have been the primary way to bless and heal for millennia.

This chapter provides several practices that may enhance your own ability to be a conduit for these healing energies. First, there is some information on using spikenard oil, thought to be the "nard" or precious ointment that Magdalene used on Jesus' head and feet. Then, the "Litany of the Magdala" is a call and a prayer to the Magdalene in her many forms. Finally, a guided visualization to France's St. Baume (Holy Balm) will put you in direct contact with Magdalene's curative and restorative energies.

USING SPIKENARD OIL IN YOUR PRACTICE

Oil of spikenard is steam distilled from the rhizomes (roots) of a plant primarily found in Nepal and India. The scent of this amber oil is described as heavy, sweet, woody and spicy, and reminiscent of patchouli. The oil is available through aromatherapy and herb shops. Spikenard oil is very intense and strong, and may be thinned with a mild oil, like sweet almond or olive oils. (Note: I recommend using diluted spikenard initally, first testing the dilution on a small patch of skin in case you have any sensitivity. Spikenard oil is only to be used externally—do not ingest this oil.)

James Twynan of the Beloved Community encourages us to approach this oil with gratitude and mindfulness. He writes, "Everything that lives has a soul, and has the power to communicate with us. In the distillation process, the soul of the plant is released and perseveved in the essential oil. The more you honor the soul of the spikenard, the more it will teach you."[22]

This is valuable advice for us as we seek to incorporate this and other essential oils into our practice.

Suggestions for using spikenard oil

Anoint your temples before sleeping to encourage dreams.

Dab some on your body before meditation, bodywork, and contemplative exercise like yoga and tai chi.

Place some in a vial and wear it around your neck as a remembrance.

Apply to your solar plexus, the center of your chest, the base of your throat, and on your forehead before beginning your daily sojourn into the world.

Put a few drops into some unscented oil and use to massage yourself or another.

A LITANY TO MARY MAGDALENE

A litany is a prayer consisting of a number of petitions. The word comes from the Latin *litania*, meaning supplication or prayer. In the litany below, we call to Magdalene for compassion and healing to flow to others as well as ourselves. Each of these lines is a jewel unto itself and may be meditated on individually for a day, a week, or a month. You may also use one or more lines of the litany as a mantra to chant while using your beads or rosary.

Litany to Mary Magdalene (A Calling to the Magdalene) [22]

By Rev. Mark Gaines

Our Lady of the Witness, intercede for us. Rose of Sharon, intercede for us.

Sangraal, intercede for us. Watchtower, intercede for us.

Matriarch of the Vine, intercede for us. Black Madonna, intercede for us.

Apostle of Apostles, intercede for us. Woman with the Alabaster Jar, intercede for us.

Daughter of Tsion, intercede for us. Our Lady of the Quest, intercede for us. Womb of Gnosis, intercede for us. Sancta Sophia, intercede for us. Dark Bride, intercede for us. Sister-Bride, intercede for us. Goddess in the Gospels, we know you. Queen of Judah, we know you. Lady of Benjamin, we know you. Our Lady of Tsion, we know you. Our Lady of Bethany, we know you. Our Lady of Gethsemane, we know you. Our Lady of Galilee, we know you. Our Lady of Seven Veils, we know you.

Our Lady of the Cross, we know you. Our Lady of the Red Egg, we know you. Our Lady of the Voyage, we know you. Our Lady of Provençe, we know you. Our Lady of Celts, we know you. Our Lady of Avalon, we know you. Our Lady of Czestochowa, we know you. Our Lady of Perpetual Help, we know you. Our Lady of Contemplation, we know you. Our Lady of the Templars, we know you.

Princess of peace, come into our world. Respite from the Sun, come into our world. Oasis in the desert, come into our world. Exposer of lies, come into our world. Breaker of hatred, come into our world. Life over death, come into our world. Queen of the Earth, come into our world. Papesse of the Church, come into our world.

Priestess among priests, come into our world. Tree of Life, come into our world. Sunset on Aries, you are among us. Exiled One of Pisces, you are among us. Kyria of Aquarius, you are among us. Our Lady of the Third Day, you are among us.

GUIDED VISUALIZATION TO THE CAVE OF ST. BAUME

In 1279, Charles, nephew of King Louis IX of France, reportedly discovered Magdalene's remains at the church of St. Maximin in Provençe. The king, who was devoted to the Magdalene, transferred the relics to the church's crypt in 1280, where they still reside. Magdalene's purported skull is in a gold reliquary and her other relics lie in a marble sarcophagus.[23] Since that time and continuing to the present, her skull is taken in a procession through the streets of St. Maximin and displayed to the throngs of enthusiastic worshippers on the occasion of her feast day. Sainte Marie-Madeleine's popularity in medieval Europe caused the town of St. Maximin to become a major pilgrimage destination. Due to the importance of this site, a basilica (a church granted special ceremonial rights by Rome) was built there in the 13th century and stands to this day, the oldest Gothic monument in Provençe.

Mary Magdalene's relics drew thousands of pilgrims to this area of France, and the chance to visit the nearby grotto of St. Baume, said to have been her hermitage for thirty years, fascinated these sojourners as well. This widely held belief recounts that the Magdalene spent long years in penance and ecstatic meditation, very much along the lines of Mary of Egypt, an early Christian ascetic.

Both the Basilica and the Grotto of St. Baume (or "Holy Balm" in French, referring to Magdalene as the bearer of precious oils) are still popular destinations today. Traditional Christianity still holds Mary Magdalene up as the supreme penitent, ever lamenting for her sins (the word "maudlin" is derived from Magdalene's name). This characterization has been reiterated by centuries of prayers, stories, and sermons.

Thankfully, many of us are now portraying the Magdalene differently, as a fully alive, sensual, powerful, and wise woman. Instead of seeing her as the ever-penitent sinner alone in her cave, becoming thinner and more enervated as the decades pass by, I have imagined her spending the years at St. Baume in quite another way. The following guided visualization is purposely not full of detail and description, so that your imagination may have a chance to fill the spaces.

Once you are ready to begin, sit or lie comfortably in an area where you will not be disturbed. After the meditation is done, come to normal waking consciousness slowly by rubbing your hands together and placing them over your closed eyes. After doing this guided visualization a few times, you may want to try working without the CD. To do this, outline the major points of the meditation, i.e., "Go up the road. Meet guide. Go to the cave." By stripping the visualization down to the essentials, you will have more liberty to journey in the imaginal realm.

LISTEN TO TRACK 1
Guided Visualization to the
Cave of Baume

You have now experienced the qualities of spikenard oil, learned the valuable prayer form of litany, and journeyed to Provençe through the guided visualization to the Cave of St. Baume. The previous three chapters have given you a solid foundation of knowledge and spiritual practice on the Magdalene Path and you are now ready to proceed to Chapter Five, where you will read about the recently revealed "Gnostic Gospels." These texts highlight Mary Magdalene as teacher and initiatrix in the spiritual life as well as the embodiment of the goddess Sophia, or Wisdom. You will learn a Gnostic form of the traditional rosary, which appears both in the text and on the CD. This chapter also offers methods of using tarot cards to intuitively access the Magdalene's wisdom, a ritual commemorating her life, and a meditation on an aspect of the Kabbalistic Tree of Life. When you finish working with Chapter Five, you will be well on your way as an initiate of the Magdalene Path. ❖

CHAPTER
FIVE

Opening to Wisdom:
The Magdalene as Initiatrix into the Mysteries

THE GOSPEL OF MARY OF MAGDALA, along with other early Christian writings not included in the New Testament, portrays the Magdalene as the most intimate companion of Yeshua and the recipient of his secret teachings of *gnosis.* The word "gnosis" literally means knowledge in Greek, and refers to the kind of knowing that only arises from a personal, unmediated experience of the Divine. There is a longstanding tradition that Jesus only imparted advanced teachings to the spiritually elite while withholding them from the masses. Connected with this supposition is the legend of two Christian lineages: the Church of Peter (the Roman Catholic Church or the Petrine Church), which spread the exoteric teachings of Jesus, and a clandestine Christian church (sometimes called the Johannine Church or the Church of

St. John), whose members are privy to Jesus' arcane teachings and are highly influenced by the Gnostic text the *Apocryphon of John* (the *Secret Book of John*).

Mary Magdalene appears in numerous ancient texts as the transmitter of this secret knowledge. In *The Gospel of Mary of Magdala*, for example, the author writes: "Peter said to Mary, 'Sister, we know that the Savior loved you more than all other women. Tell us the words of the Savior that you remember, the things which you know that we don't because we haven't heard them.' Mary responded, 'I will teach you about what is hidden from you.'" (6:1–4)[24] This important gospel depicts the Magdalene as an enlightened teacher and the leader of Yeshua's disciples after his death.

Fragments of a Coptic translation of the *Gospel of Mary of Magdala* first came to light in the late 19th century, and more small pieces of the gospel, this time in Greek, appeared in 1917 and 1983. (For a detailed history of these finds, I recommend reading Karen L. King's *The Gospel of Mary of Magdala: Jesus and the First Woman Apostle*.) Scholars date the oldest version to the early 3rd century and think that these fragments may represent only a portion, perhaps half, of the original text. Nevertheless, what we have is revolutionary, especially for those of us who only know of Mary Magdalene through New Testament stories and perhaps Sunday school catechisms.

Another significant Gnostic book is the *Pistis Sophia*, dated by scholars circa 250–300 CE. The *Pistis Sophia* (Faith of Sophia or Faith Wisdom) echoes this exalted vision of Mary Magdalene. At one point in this manuscript, Jesus says to her: "Blessed Mary, you whom I shall complete with all the mysteries on high, speak openly, for you are one whose heart is set on heaven's kingdom more than all your brothers."[25] At the conclusion of the *Pistis Sophia*, Jesus marvels at Mary Magdalene's wisdom and says: "Well done, Mary, pure spiritual woman."[26] Yet another Gnostic document, the *Gospel of Philip*, states, "The companion of the (savior) is Mary Magdalene. The (savior loved) her more than (all) the disciples, (and he) kissed her often on her (mouth)."[27] These are only some of the ancient writings acclaiming Mary Magdalene as a spiritual leader and an essential member of Jesus' group of disciples.

In addition, Magdalene's elevated position is highlighted by the New Testament gospel story where Jesus frees her from seven demons. The New Testament allusion to seven devils most probably indicates Mary Magdalene's high state of spiritual development. In order to understand this, we need to place the incident into the cultural context of the early Christians.

In their world, the number seven possessed great power and significance. Considered sacred in antiquity, the number seven was called the "perfect number" by the Pythagoreans and is the most frequently mentioned number in the Bible. The ancients watched the seven visible planets moving across the firmament of fixed stars and developed their cosmology around this observation. "From antiquity until Copernicus, the universe was popularly believed to consist of a great celestial hierarchy reaching from the earth, up through the spheres of the seven planetary gods (Moon, Mercury, Venus, Sun Mars, Jupiter, and Saturn), to the fixed sphere of the timeless and unchanging stars."[28] Based on this cosmology, philosophical schools such as the Neo-Platonists and certain Gnostic groups envisioned the soul progressing through these seven planes in order to reach perfection.

Caitlin Matthews writes in *Sophia: Goddess of Wisdom, Bride of God:* "Jesus frequently exorcises the sick of such possession, but it is not without significance that Mary should possess seven devils—the very same number of planetary rulers that have to be overcome by the Gnostic initiate. This statement establishes Mary as someone who has already reached perfection, according to the Gnostic ideal."[29] In this view, the healing of Magdalene is an initiation into completeness and perfection, an interpretation that stands at odds with what most of us were taught.

Perhaps what is most striking about these different texts is the great contrast between their views of the Magdalene and the image promulgated by the Church over the millennia. Clearly many Christians in the early centuries of the movement believed Mary Magdalene to be an incarnation of Sophia (Wisdom) and an exalted "way-shower," someone who illuminates and is an exemplar of the spiritual path. Due to the modern discovery and circulation of these ancient manuscripts, Western culture is re-imagining her as a teacher or a high priestess. Those on the Magdalene Path may approach her in any of these roles to assist them on their journey.

One potent way to meet the Magdalene on the inner planes is to work with tarot cards. I find that the Magdalene manifests in different tarot cards, and you will need to shuffle through your deck to find the cards that resonate with your images of her. There are many ways in which to incorporate the cards into your practice, including meditation, ritual, and by visualizing yourself entering any card's scenario and interacting with the characters. Mary Greer's *Tarot for Your Self* is a wonderful guidebook to using tarot for personal transformation.

The first card that I connect to the Magdalene is the High Priestess, second in the series of major trump cards. In traditional decks, the High Priestess is veiled and mysterious and holds a rolled parchment signifying hidden knowledge. An archetype of wisdom and gnosis, she sits on a throne between two columns, named Jakin and Boaz, which were the main pillars at King Solomon's temple in Jerusalem. These pillars also recall the High Priestess's connection with ancient goddesses, such as Isis, and their places of worship. In this card, Mary Magdalene as the High Priestess is the embodiment of *Chokmah*, the figure of Wisdom mentioned often in the Hebrew Bible, as well as the Shekhinah, the Hebrew term for the divine indwelling feminine. Her presence between the two pillars symbolizes the perfect balance of polarized energies, such as force and form, light and dark, and severity and mercy. In the Jewish Kabbalah, the second divine emanation (these emanations are called *sephirot* in Hebrew) is called Chokmah, the Hebrew word for wisdom. The Hebrew Bible thus refers to wisdom as Chokmah (the initial consonant is pronounced with a guttural "ch" like the German "Bach"). It is no coincidence that the Kabbalistic Chokmah and the tarot card of the High Priestess are both second in their respective schemas and both are linked to the Magdalene.

I also imagine Mary Magdalene strongly linked to the Hierophant card, in her role as initiatrix into the mysteries. The card, sometimes called the Papesse or the Psychopomp, is fifth among the twenty-two major trumps. While some may interpret the Hierophant as a male representative of patriarchal religion, I envision this figure more positively along the lines of a psychopomp. *Psychopompos* is a Greek word meaning "one who conducts souls to the afterworld." From a wider perspective, this person or deity guides souls on the inner paths and assists them in moving through liminal realms like those of birth, death, and initiation.

Sometimes the psychopomp may act as a gatekeeper, refusing to allow an initiate to pass through the High Priestess's pillars of wisdom without proof of their spiritual maturity. In this role, the psychopomp may take on a fierce and terrifying aspect, testing the candidate's resolve to deal with the unconscious and castaway parts of their psyche before advancing to the next level of the spiritual journey. The Magdalene in her role of teacher, wise woman, and Dark Goddess perfectly fulfills this characterization of a psychopomp.

In the tarot, the Magdalene also manifests in the World Card, the twenty-first and final trump card of the major arcana. Traditionally this card shows a beautiful naked woman dancing in the center of a circle or wreath, surrounded by symbols of the four elements. Holding the caduceus (winged staff) of Mercury, she embodies the achievement of final transmutation at all levels. This exuberant goddess portrays the Soul of the World, the Anima Mundi, as she is made whole and complete, incorporating all aspects of the world and the self. Mary Magdalene in her role as Sophia, or Wisdom, offers us a way out of ignorance and delusion to a fully conscious and integrated selfhood.

Other practices in this chapter are designed to invoke the Magdalene who embodies spiritual knowledge and is representative of the mysteries. The first is a ritual called "A Gnostic Commemoration of Mary Magdalene," a theatrical ceremony to be performed on the Magdalene's feast day of July 22. But you may use this ritual at any time of the year to good effect, and one person or several may enact this sacred drama.

Another practice is the "Holy Gnostic Rosary," which is composed along the traditional lines of the Roman Catholic rosary, but employs Gnostic theology and symbolism to create a dynamic and remarkable set of prayers. The imagery in this version of the rosary draws on symbology that may be unfamiliar to you. For more information on Gnostic myths and conceptions, refer to Stephan A. Hoeller's book *Gnosticism: New Light on the Ancient Tradition of Inner Knowing*.

As with any of the prayers and rituals in this book, you should feel free to modify it by substituting inclusive pronouns or choosing to employ other names for the Divine. You may also wish to use traditional rosary beads to recite the prayers. Directions on using a rosary are available in many books: take a look at the Our Lady of Guadalupe web site or Liz Kelly's book *The Rosary: A Path into Prayer*.

A guided meditation on *Tipherath*, one of the ten *sephiroth* or divine emanations of the Kabbalistic Tree of Life, rounds out the practices. This simple meditation is designed to connect you with the radiance, power, and balance typified by this particular expression of the Holy and introduces the yoga of the sun to your practice.

A GNOSTIC COMMEMORATION OF MARY MAGDALENE: A CELEBRATION OF LOVE AND FAITHFULNESS [30]

By Soror Lucia

Celebrants

This ritual was designed to be flexible in regards to the number of people needed to perform it. Listed below are all of the parts to be read. One person, two people, etc., may read the parts. Someone sitting offside can read any of the non-narrative parts, or be dressed in full costume standing around the primary Celebrant.

Primary Celebrant, who acts as narrator; Jesus; Simon Peter; unnamed disciple; Andrew; and Mary Magdalene.

Tools

Everyone present should be instructed to bring their own candles to light, or small candles with wax-catchers should be provided for all. In addition, you will need a fire censer (or incense burner); water cup; skull (or a representation); a book; a red-colored egg; an unguent jar (or perfume bottle); a large altar candle, unlit; an altar cloth (robin-egg blue or red); and five dark-colored cloths and a dark robe with sash (to make six over-garments in all), to be worn by the Celebrant over a shining white robe/gown.

The altar should be arranged with the skull sitting on the open book, with the fire censer on the right and the water cup on the left. The candle should sit behind the book, and the perfume jar and red egg should be placed in any position where they can be seen.

Celebrant stands on East side of the altar, facing West.

CELEBRANT: "Let us gather to remember Mary Magdalene, the woman who loved Christ greatest of all. She, who was the most earnest of his admirers, she who was his dearest companion, she who was said to receive his kisses on her mouth.

"Let this place be consecrated and purified as we prepare to bless the name of Mary Magdalene."

Celebrant takes fire censer, and turns to go directly to the East, then to each of the other three directions. At each station, she forms an equal-armed cross. When she returns to the East, she holds the censer high and says,

"As the angel burned brightly at the tomb, so may this space be consecrated by holy fire."

She then turns and goes directly back to the East side of the altar, replacing the censer. Then, she takes the water cup and turns to go directly to the East, then to each of the other three directions again. At each station, she sprinkles water in the form of an equal armed cross. When she returns to the East, she holds the cup high and says:

"As the river Jordan renewed the lives of those who followed, so may this space be purified by blessed water."

She then turns and goes directly back to the East side of the altar, replacing the water cup.

CELEBRANT: "Be thou revered and honored!

"Blessed teacher of teachers,

"Servant in the work of wisdom!

"Patron of the faithful who find joy to counter sorrow,

"Lovely sister formed of grace, mercy, and righteousness!

"Be with us now, this day and this hour, as we come together to bless your name and memory.

"With the Divine Unknowable and your brother and sisters of the Pleroma, we stand in community with you.

"The eons and angels who populate the heavens exist in harmony; you are the flesh of Sophia, one half of an earthly unit as she is one half of an immortal unit. You embody the work of Zoë, the daughter who was sent to kindle the flame of wisdom in each of us.

"In your faithfulness, you were relieved of seven demons sprung from the injuries to your heart and soul. May we always remember to exchange our garments of darkness for a vestment of shining light as we journey toward the eternal."

Celebrant circumambulates, moving sunwise around the altar, spiraling outward toward the West, where she sheds one of her cloths. She then sheds a cloth at the North, then East, then South, then West again, then North, then finally discards her black robe at the East, revealing her shining white gown. She circles the space one more time, spiraling in to the center of the room again to the East side of the altar. This circumambulation represents rising from the darkness into the light, as well as shedding our heavier bodies for the more subtle.

CELEBRANT: "The task of seeing the stone rolled away fell to you, and as you saw the tomb was empty you becried your fate. Our passion becomes your passion, your sorrow at being separated from the master of your heart."

MAGDALENE: "Death! Thief! Oh, unfeeling God!"

JESUS: "Why do you then seek the living among the dead, Mary?"

MAGDALENE: "Rabboni! Love is alive!"

As Celebrant exclaims "Rabboni," she can fall to her knees in reverence, or remain standing. Some gesture should be made to drive home what an intense moment it was to realize that her love, whom she believed was dead, was now alive. She should also lean toward or move toward Jesus (if someone is playing the part of Jesus) in a movement to perhaps embrace him, but he stops her.

JESUS: "Noli me tangere."

If someone is playing the role of Jesus, he should hold up his hand in a "stop" gesture. He is saying, "Touch me not," so obviously, he is trying to prevent her from touching him. If possible, Magdalene will look disappointed that she cannot touch him.

CELEBRANT: "Without delay, you ran to the hiding place of the disciples to tell them what you had seen and heard through grace. And your burden became heavy when they did not believe."

UNNAMED DISCIPLE: "Surely these are the idle tales of women!"

CELEBRANT: "You secured in your heart the words of your Lord, who imparted to you many things. And as you conveyed his words to his followers, again you were doubted."

ANDREW: "I, at least, do not believe that the Savior said these things. For certainly these teachings are strange ideas."

CELEBRANT: "And even the Master who proclaimed that women are also seekers of life and eternal wisdom had to defend you against your brothers."

SIMON PETER: "Make Mary leave us, for women are not worthy of life!"

CELEBRANT: "Our brothers were asleep as the task of Sophia was worked. But you stayed awake in the darkest night, with the song of perseverance on your tongue and your consort in your deepest soul.

"Therefore, we remember you in these symbols:"

Celebrant holds up each item in turn, looking upward with them.

"The jar of perfume, which you carried to anoint the dead body of your love and master.

"The egg, which turned red as you spoke of the Divine.

"Books, which you studied in solitude, for the path of gnosis was one of reunification.

"The skull, which you meditated upon as a symbol of rebirth and renewal. For through death, you gained a greater understanding of life.

"May you rekindle the eternal flame for us this night, and make us more easily seen by angels, themselves invisible, as we light candles to honor your love and faithfulness. This we do under the veil of earthly things as we strive toward unity."

As the Celebrant says, "As we light candles . . . ," she lights the big candle on the altar. Celebrant then directs everyone present to light their candle by the flame of the large candle on the altar and to meditate on the symbols thereon. All remain standing after lighting their candles.

CELEBRANT: "Let us invoke the Mother of the Universe:

"O Gentle, O Kind, O Blessed Sophia,

"Thy children on earth call to thee.

"We pray thee, Beloved Mother, to cast forth

"Thy net of woven starlight.

"Fling it wide across the ocean of the universe

"And gather us home to the realms of Light.

"May we be as loving and faithful as our venerable sister, Mary Magdalene, may she never be forgotten, and may her name be eternally blessed.

"Amen.

"Thank you for joining in this commemoration of the Magdalene. This concludes our ritual. You are welcome to take home the candles that you've lit here tonight."

Celebrant then extinguishes the large candle on the altar.

THE HOLY GNOSTIC ROSARY [31]

by Rev. John Goelz and Rev. Steven Marshall

The Order of the Recitation of the Holy Gnostic Rosary

1. The Sign of the Cross and the Gnostic's Creed
2. The Gnostic's Prayer
3. Hail Sophia three times
4. Gloria Patri
5. Announce the First Mystery: then say the Gnostic's Prayer
6. Hail Sophia ten times, while meditating on the Mystery
7. Gloria Patri
8. Announce the Second Mystery, then say the Gnostic's Prayer
9. Hail Sophia ten times, while meditating on the Mystery
10. Gloria Patri
11. Announce the third Mystery: then say the Gnostic's Prayer
12. Hail Sophia ten times, while meditating on the Mystery
13. Gloria Patri
14. Announce the fourth Mystery: then say the Gnostic's Prayer
15. Hail Sophia ten times, while meditating on the Mystery
16. Gloria Patri
17. Announce the fifth Mystery: then say the Gnostic's Prayer
18. Hail Sophia ten times, while meditating on the Mystery
19. Closing prayer

The Sign of the Cross

In the name of the Unknown Father, in Truth, Mother of all,
in union and redemption and sharing of the powers,
peace to all on whom this name reposes.

The Gnostic's Creed

I acknowledge one great invisible God, unrevealable,
unmarked, ageless and unproclaimable; the unknown Father,
the eon of the eons, who brought forth in the silence
with his providence: the Father, the Mother, and the Son.
I acknowledge the Christos, the self-begotten living son,
the glory of the Father and the virtue of the Mother,
who given birth from the virginal and ineffable mother
was made incarnate, the Perfect one. Who in the word of
the Great Invisible God, came down from above to annul
the emptiness of this age and restore the fullness to the eon.
I acknowledge the Holy Spirit, the Bride of the Christos,
the Mother of the Eons, the great virginal and ineffable
Mother who proceeded from herself a gift of Herself out of
the silence of the Unknown God.
I acknowledge the Light of the one church in every place:
Interior, Invisible, Secret, and Universal,
the foundation of the lights of the great living God.
I seek liberation of my perfection from the corruptions
of the world and look to the gathering of the sparks of Light
from the sea of forgetfulness.
Amen.

LISTEN TO TRACK 2
The Holy Gnostic Rosary

The Gnostic's Prayer

Almighty God, whose footstool is the highest firmament:
Great Ruler of Heaven, and all the powers therein:
Hear the prayers of Thy Servants, who put their trust in Thee.

We pray Thee, supply our needs from day to day: command Thy
heavenly host to comfort and succor us:

That it may be to Thy glory and unto the good of man.

Forgive us our transgressions as we forgive our brothers and sisters:
be present with us: strengthen and sustain us:

For we are but instruments in Thy hands.

Let us not fall into temptation: defend us from all danger and evil:

Let Thy mighty power ever guard and protect us.

Thou great fount of knowledge and Wisdom:

Instruct Thy servants by Thy holy presence:

Guide and support us, now and forever.

Amen.

Hail Sophia

Hail Sophia, full of light, the Christ is with thee,
blessed art thou among all the eons, and blessed is the liberator
of thy light, Jesus. Holy Sophia, Mother of all gods, pray to
the Light for us thy children, now and in the hour of our death.
Amen.

Gloria Patri

Glory be to the Father, and to the Son, and to the Holy Spirit.

As it was in the beginning, is now, and ever shall be,

unto the eons of eons.

Amen.

The First Gnostic Mystery: The Assumption of Sophia

Hail to the Great Savior, for He has lifted the Soul and the Heart of the Heavens out of the prisonhouse of matter and raised Her up into the Pleroma.

The Second Gnostic Mystery: The Coronation of Sophia

And the Lord gave unto Sophia a crown with twelve stars which are the lights of redemption and the Throne of Manifestation for Her seat, and He also gave unto Her the Cross of Mystery as a scepter by which she shall rule the Eons.

The Third Gnostic Mystery: The Renunciation

And the Lord laid the Kingdom at Her feet, and renounced all sovereignty and rule unto Her Throne. The sword that he brought he received at her hands, to redeem and to conquer for the reception of the Light.

The Fourth Gnostic Mystery: The Bride Chamber

"My Soul doth magnify the Lord, for a lowly handmaid hath been found perfected in Sophia and the King is come. Be it done according to thy Word."

The King answered and said, "Arise, O Daughter of the Light, and enter into thy rest."

The Fifth Gnostic Mystery: The Descent of the New Jerusalem

Behold, a small star from the Heavens descends to the earth,

With Light more brilliant than the Sun.

It comes to dwell in the Hearts of the children of men, and these hearts are the foundation upon which is built the Eternal City, New Jerusalem.

Closing Prayer

O Gentle, O Kind, O Blessed Sophia,
Thy children on earth call unto Thee.

We pray Thee, Beloved Mother, to cast forth
thy net of woven starlight.
Fling it wide across the ocean of the universe
to gather us home to the realms of Light.
Amen.

KABBALISTIC MEDITATION ON TIPHERATH

The emanation of divine energy called Tipherath (pronounced ti-FAIR-it)
occupies the central position in the Kabbalistic Tree of Life and correlates
with the center of our bodies, the heart, and solar plexus regions. (I suggest
Omraam Mikhaël Aïvanhov's book *The Fruits of the Tree of Life: The Cabbalistic
Tradition,* for more general information on this subject.) The Hebrew word
"Tipherath" means beauty or splendor, and this sphere manifests the qualities of harmony, integrity, and balance. Michael is the reigning archangel of
Tipherath, and the *Malachim* is the resident angelic order. Tipherath's color
is yellow, its metal is gold, and its visible symbol is the sun.

Omraam Mikhaël Aïvanhov (1900–1987), a Bulgarian spiritual teacher,
taught that the solar orb is a symbol for the Christos energy as well as a
manifestation of Tipherath. Following in the Platonic tradition, Aïvanhov
conceived of the sun—indeed, the entire universe—as being alive, intelligent,
and ensouled. He recommended practicing a sunrise meditation each dawn
between the vernal and autumnal equinoxes, the time when the subtle energy
or *prana* of the solar rays is considered to be most potent.

Directly working with the sun via prayer and contemplation is very
effective, even if it is not done at sunrise. According to Aïvanhov, conscious assimilation of the sun's gentle morning rays has inestimable benefit
to our physical and spiritual well-being. And calling to mind the Gnostic

view of the Christos energy consisting both of Christ the Logos (Jesus) and Christ the Sophia (Magdalene), we can meditate on the sun as a powerful aid to invoking both masculine and feminine aspects of the Christ energy. (To protect your vision it is important to never look directly at the sun, however.)

Invocation to the Sun

To be repeated silently as the first rays of the sunrise become visible.

As the sun rises over the world, so may the Sun of Truth, Freedom, Immortality, and Eternity rise in my spirit!

As the sun rises above the world, so may the Sun of Love and Immensity rise in my soul!

As the sun rises above the world, so may the Sun of Intelligence, Light, and Wisdom rise in my intellect!

As the sun rises above the world, so may the Sun of gentleness, kindness, joy, happiness, and purity rise in my heart!

As the luminous, radiant sun rises over the world, so may the Sun of strength, power, force, dynamic energy, and activity rise in my will!

And as this luminous, radiant, living sun rises over the world, so may the Sun of health, vitality, and vigour rise in my body! [32]

By engaging in these practices, you have become familiar with aspects of the Gnostic Christian tradition, as well as prayers, meditation, and ritual that draw upon their ancient texts. You have also dipped your foot into the vast ocean of Kabbalah, a tradition of Jewish mysticism that extends back millennia, and learned a simple and expedient meditation to increase your energy and centeredness.

In Chapter Six we arrive at the final set of meditations, whose focal point is Mary Magdalene as the Dark Goddess. First, you will become acquainted with the historical and mythological connections between the Magdalene and other Dark Goddesses. Subsequently, you will listen to a modern Gnostic guided visualization initiating you into a relationship with Magdalene as the "Fiery Bride." Following this visualization is another encounter recorded on the CD, featuring the Magdalene as Grail Guardian, set in Glastonbury, England (thought to be the ancient isle of Avalon). *Invoking Mary Magdalene* ends with an evocative and potent ritual calling on the energies of the Dark Goddess in her many guises. These practices are among the most revelatory and intense of any included in this book. ✤

CHAPTER
SIX

Accessing Power:
Encountering the Magdalene as Dark Goddess

I am black and beautiful.
Song of Songs 1:5

CAVES, GROTTOES, CRYPTS, wells, crossroads, and the underworld—these are the sorts of places in which the Dark Goddesses dwell
and reign. Locales that are damp, earthy, fecund, mysterious, and hidden
are their natural haunts. These chthonic (or deities of the underworld)
divinities appear all over the world, identified by a plethora of names
and, not infrequently, show up as sinister figures in our nightmares and
ghost stories. The Irish have the *Cailleach,* the Old Hag; in Scotland, the
Washerwoman (or the Woman at the Ford) rinses bloody clothes in a river

and prophesies death; Lilith, Adam's first wife and a fertility goddess of the Near East, is rumored even today to steal Jewish children from their mothers; and Hel is the Scandinavian Queen of the Underworld. Western fairy tales are replete with characters typifying the negative Dark Goddess, such as the Bad Fairy, the Wicked Witch, the Evil Stepmother, and Baba Yaga. In the Arthurian romances, we have Kundry, also known as the Loathly Lady or Loathly Damsel.

Very rarely, though, do we see these shadowy feminine figures in a positive way, as role models to emulate and powerful goddesses to revere. It was not always this way, contends Demetra George, in her book *Mysteries of the Dark Moon: The Healing Power of the Dark Goddess*. In earlier cultures, writes George: "The Dark Goddess, who is the embodiment of the dark phase of the moon's cycle, was thus honored for her role in presiding over the mysteries and initiations of the intermediary passage between death and rebirth … The ancient power of the Dark Goddess's capacity to heal, regenerate, and renew was centered in her ecstatic spirituality."[33] George remarks that the skills and arts associated with this Goddess and with women in general—such as astrology, magic, alchemy, and midwifery—eventually came under suspicion by the increasingly male-dominated church, and they remain so today. In the early days of Christianity, women held leadership positions such as bishops, deacons, and preachers. But by 200 CE, "we have no evidence for women taking prophetic, priestly, and episcopal roles among orthodox churches."[34] By demonizing menstruation, childbirth, and traditional herbal medicine, the Church tamped down women's enormous power as bringers of life, containing it beneath a stifling code of religious restrictions, civil laws, and social decorum.

As women's authority in the Church waned, the veneration of Mary, the mother of Jesus, and the attendant virtue of virginity gained ascendancy. By the 4th century, the Church held up virginity and chastity as lofty virtues, and encouraged Marian devotions while simultaneously decrying the ancient goddess religions.[35] The 4th-century bishop Augustine of Hippo railed against goddess worship in his treatise *The City of God*, pointing out that her worship flourished even in his time.[36]

Not only were the goddess cults still alive in the Near East in the first centuries of the Church, they also spread across Europe with the Roman conquest. Worship of the Roman mother goddess Cybele thrived in Lyons, France, three centuries after the birth of Jesus. Eventually Lyons became the center of Christianity in France, and a shrine housing a Black Madonna replaced Cybele's hilltop temple.[37] In Paris, the dark Egyptian divinity Isis held court as the most prominent goddess, and elsewhere in France, the populace worshipped the magnificent Greek goddess Artemis of Ephesus, often depicted as a black deity.[38] Her temple in Ephesus, now in ruins, was one of the seven wonders of the ancient world. Contemporaneous with the imported Roman and Greek divinities were the native European goddesses revered by the indigenous populace, like Brigit in Ireland, Freyja in Scandinavia, and Ostara in the Germanic lands.

Where does Mary Magdalene fit into all of this? She has become the Christian Dark Goddess, carrying the cast-off, shadow attributes such as sexuality and independence that the Church eradicated from their characterization of the Virgin Mary. When we compare the Church's image of the Blessed Virgin—pure, virginal, chaste, submissive—to the regal, fiery, and sensual Near Eastern goddesses like Cybele and Astarte, she can appear insipid, powerless, and one-dimensional. Mary exhibits no lust, pride, overindulgence, or dominant propensities; she is the wholly compliant woman who is not divine, but also not quite human. According to the Catholic doctrine of the Immaculate Conception, the Blessed Virgin is set apart from all other mortals because she alone was conceived without sin.

On the other hand, Mary Magdalene is highly sexualized in the Christian mythos. Her golden-red hair flowing wildly around her symbolizes her passion and sexual nature. While the Virgin Mary is always shown completely clothed, the Magdalene is frequently depicted in various states of undress or in the nude, sometimes quite provocatively. She is the independently wealthy woman of the Gospels, who is not under the control of a father, husband, or son. In order to disable this powerful woman in the eyes of the faithful, the Church cast her in the role of prostitute, who is only saved from her sins by submitting to her male savior. Furthermore, the early Christian texts extolling Magdalene as a highly advanced spiritual teacher and leader in her community were discredited and destroyed.

By exterminating sexuality, earthiness, and power from the image of the Virgin Mary, Western culture forced those attributes previously held by the great goddesses to the substrata of culture. If the Dark Goddess is not acknowledged consciously, she will manifest unconsciously in harmful societal patterns. Hilary Hart comments that: "The Dark Feminine is the ground of all being, an elemental dimension of creation. We cannot cut ourselves off from it because it exists everywhere. But if we deny it a place in our individual and cultural consciousness, if we resist and denigrate it, this energy will continue to manifest in our lives through cycles of starvation and overindulgence and we will be left spinning within collective patterns of desolation and isolation."[39]

By the Middle Ages, the cult of the Virgin Mary grew exponentially, fanned by the Church's encouragement. As if to compensate for this fact, devotion to

Mary Magdalene also increased greatly, making her the most popular saint of that time. There are three great pilgrimages for Christians: Rome, Jerusalem, and Santiago de Compostela in Spain. In the medieval period, the city of Vézelay, France, the purported resting place of the Magdalene's relics, became the fourth most important destination for pilgrims.[40]

As previously mentioned, this is the same period of greatest growth for the European Black Madonnas. It is fascinating to note that author Ean Begg states that Black Virgin shrines exist in at least fifty churches dedicated to the Magdalene, primarily in France.[41] While most of us may assume that Black Madonnas are depictions of the Virgin Mary holding the child Jesus, this may not necessarily be the case. Some scholars, including Begg, trace the Black Madonnas to the Middle Eastern goddess worship, especially that of Isis and Diana. Legends that have circulated for centuries claim that the Knights Templar, a medieval Catholic order of warriors active in the Holy Land Crusades, brought a number of Black Virgin deities home from their Near Eastern travels. The crypt of Chartres cathedral, along with those of numerous other Gothic churches, contains a Black Madonna shrine. Chartres' underground vault not only houses one of the Black Virgins of Chartres, known as "Notre Dame Sous Terre" (Our Lady Underground), but also a sacred well dating back to Druidic times.

There is speculation that some of the Black Madonna statues portray Mary Magdalene with her child, the fruit of her marriage with Jesus. While we may never be able to prove that the Magdalene is embodied in some of the Black Madonna deities, it is possible that for some Christians, especially in Provençe, she became conflated with the Black Virgins in the popular imagination. Provençe, a region located in the southwest of France, was also the stronghold of the Cathars, a group of dissident Christians who were deemed heretical by the Catholic Church and were massacred by the thousands in the High Middle Ages. Margaret Starbird believes that the Cathars, whose doctrines paralleled the early Christian Gnostics in many ways, revered Mary Magdalene as the bride of Jesus. Starbird's provocative research, detailed in her book *The Woman with the Alabaster Jar*, lays out a riveting narrative tracing the possible connections between the Magdalene, the Cathars, the troubadours, and the courts of love, as well as the origins of the French tarot.

Finally, the Black Virgin may be connected metaphorically to the initial part of the alchemist's sacred work, that of the *nigredo* (Latin for "blackness"). During this phase, the substance to be transformed is placed in a vessel and heated over fire, causing it to become blackened and putrefied. The nigredo, while inherently a destructive process, is essential for the final purification and transformation of the original substance. Likewise, we may view the Dark Goddess both as a figure of death and ruin as well as an emblem of renewal and rebirth.

While these historical and mythological explorations are absorbing, we need to connect them to those of us today who are traveling on the Magdalene Path. It seems to me that one of our goals must be to fully express and celebrate our embodied nature, independence, power, and eroticism. To show forth the Dark Goddess as she was originally understood—delighting in her senses and those of her lovers, guiding souls through liminal places and across thresholds, healing and nurturing, as well as cutting through deeply held illusions and shattering the bonds of egotism. Jungian analysts Marion Woodman and Elinor Dickson express this idea beautifully: "The freedom we seek does not lie in the patriarchal control we so desperately attempt to maintain. Rather it lies in letting go ... Letting go is embracing the Black

Goddess, she who will open our eyes to our illusions … Descending into her territory demands the death of a rigidly controlled life."[42]

The practices in this chapter offer the possibility of contacting that deep feminine energy that has been repressed so long in all of us. In one sense, it may be somewhat frightening to dance with the Dark Goddess: she is capricious, wild, a trickster of the highest order, and bound to no one's rules or moral order. But engaging her archetype is necessary in the quest to become an integrated human being, whether you are a male or female.

One extraordinary way to begin working with the Dark Goddess is through the medium of art. For example, a few years ago, I signed up for a "Spirit Doll" workshop at a local Boulder arts center. In this day-long session, the teacher, Boulder artist Isolde Hathaway, showed us how to create a doll using intuition and contemplation to guide the process of working with the socks, fabric scraps, and found objects we used as our materials. She started us off by dumping a huge bag of old socks in a riot of colors out on the studio floor and told us to let the socks draw us to them, rather than the other way around. A black paisley pair of ankle-length women's socks called to me. Once we finished the first step of constructing the sock doll's body, we meditated on how our spirit doll would like to be dressed, what sort of hair seemed right, and so on.

The results surprised me. A statuesque black doll emerged from my hands without my conscious planning. Her silk clothes in bright tropical colors clung to her generous curves, and a spiral button sewn at her solar plexus indicated her power center. She was bald, sported dangling earrings, beaded bracelets, and a serpent crown topped with a fat piece of carnelian stone. In case she needed to conduct rituals in the nude, her clothes, which were secured with Velcro, could be removed.

As I held her, she seemed to communicate that she was a priestess of Sekhmet, one of the most powerful goddesses in the Egyptian pantheon. I knew little about this lion-faced goddess at the time. Later, I found out that Sekhmet always wears a crown decorated with the cobra-shaped *uraeus*, indicating her sovereignty and enlightened consciousness. For weeks she rode in the passenger seat of my car and sat on my desk at work; I did not want to be parted from her. I bring up my Priestess of Sekhmet doll because it was one of the first times that the Dark Goddess directly manifested in my life. Since then, my devotional practices center around different refractions of this Dark Goddess, who is to me a deep well of wisdom and fearlessness.

For those who would like to craft their own spirit dolls, I have included books and web sites in the Additional Resources section that address the general topic of soft doll-making. Be on the lookout for doll classes and workshops hosted by craft shops and bead and fiber festivals.

UNION WITH THE HOLY BRIDE (ST. MARY MAGDALENE) GUIDED MEDITATION [43]

By Tau Malachi

Our first practice is a guided visualization of the Holy Bride, as Sophian Gnostic tradition that refers to Mary Magdalene. Tau Malachi—a Gnostic Christian teacher in the Sophian tradition and author of numerous books on spirituality—introduces this very potent meditation with a few words about the Magdalene's prominence in Sophian Gnostic theology:

LISTEN TO TRACK 3
Union with the Holy Bride

> *The Holy Bride has many Faces, both Bright and Dark. One the one hand, she is the Maiden of Light, the Mother of the Royal Blood, and Crone of Ageless Wisdom; on the other hand, she is Lilith, Naamah, and Iggaret (Mistress of the Night, Queen*

of Demons, and Hag of Chaos). Thus, the Holy Bride has many forms and there are many different practices associated with her in the [Sophian] Tradition—Peaceful, Blissful and Wrathful ... [O]ne does not need an initiation from anyone to contact the Bride. One need only desire to experience her and consciously invoke her and she will come, in one form or another, according to one's own capacity to receive her. [44]

MAGDALENE AS GRAIL GUARDIAN AND QUEEN OF SHADOWS MEDITATION

The small market town of Glastonbury in southwestern England is the setting for the next meditation. Thought to be a holy center since the Megalithic era, it draws people from all over the world to walk its hallowed paths and stroll the ancient monastery ruins, drink from the healing Chalice Well waters, and soak up the indescribable soul-force that pervades the town.

LISTEN TO TRACK 4
Magdalene as Grail Guardian and Queen of Shadows Meditation

Strolling down the town's main thoroughfare, Magdalen Street, you come to a medieval gate that leads to the heart of Glastonbury, the ruins of the medieval Abbey. Legend relates that Joseph of Arimathea, Mother Mary, Mary Magdalene, and other followers of Jesus landed at Glastonbury after escaping or being exiled from the Holy Land after the crucifixion. Glastonbury is also thought to be the earthly site of Avalon, as well as the resting place of the Holy Grail, and thus holds a prominent place in the Arthurian tales. In this practice, you will travel to Glastonbury and work with Magdalene as Dark Goddess and Guardian of the Grail.

RITUAL EVOKING THE DARK GODDESS
IN HER MYRIAD FORMS [45]

A ritual evoking the Dark Goddess in her forms as Sekhmet, Kali, Lilith, and Magdalene rounds out this chapter. As was mentioned earlier, Sekhmet is a potent Egyptian goddess, whose sphere of influence includes war, magic, and the healing arts. We discussed the Hindu goddess Kali in the second chapter; she is the fearsome warrior queen and consort of the god Shiva. Lilith is an ancient Near Eastern goddess who originally manifested as a beautiful young girl and handmaiden to Inanna, a prominent fertility goddess worshipped by the Sumerians and Babylonians. In Jewish texts, Lilith appears as the first wife of Adam and refused to be subservient to her husband and was thus cast out of Eden. Jewish folklore still regards her as the embodiment of feminine evil, a demon who attacks children and imperils birthing women, creating a cautionary figure of a woman who challenges male authority.

You may do this ritual as part of a group or by yourself. It is best performed during the evening hours, although it may be done during the day if necessary. Decorate your altar, which should be facing the north, with fiery colors such as yellow, red, orange, and magenta; brightly colored flowers; and representations of animals sacred to the Dark Goddess, such as snakes, crocodiles, owls, and ravens. You will also need a photograph, print, statue, or a tarot card that portrays a Dark Goddess for each participant.

The ceremony starts with the group arrayed in a standing circle. Those participants representing the Dark Goddesses stand in their respective quarters of the circle: Kali stands in the north; Lilith, the west; Sekhmet, the south; and Mary Magdalene in the east. The person acting as the Celebrant may stand anywhere in the ring.

CELEBRANT: "Our intention is to journey to the realm of the Dark One, who is known as Persephone, Hecate, Durga, Cailleach (kal-yak), Isis, Ereshkigal, and by countless other titles from time immemorial. We ask for the favor and blessing of the Dark One as we seek to reclaim our innate power, wisdom, and energy from behind the veils of illusion."

KALI: "Guardians of the North, be with us as we voyage to through shadowy passages to unknown realms."

LILITH: "Guardians of the West, be with us as we descend to the depths of the arctic sea."

SEKHMET: "Guardians of the South, be with us as we run through dazzling streams of fire."

MAGDALENE: "Guardians of the East, be with us as the wild and capricious winds carry us."

CELEBRANT: "We invoke the Dark One, whose breasts mirror a luminous star band, whose belly radiates power, and who glows as phosphorescence in the shadows. O Dark One, you are the origin of all magic and incantations, of all alchemy and healing and impenetrable secrets. Soothing rays of benediction emanate your lotus palms even as you sever our illusions with your razor-sharp sword. It is to you, O Dark One, we call. Tonight we summon forth deeply ingrained negative patterns that no longer serve us, in order that they may be transformed. We offer them and ourselves to you. O Kali, Who Wears a Garland of Skulls; O Sekhmet, Bearer of the Thunderbolt; O Lilith, Queen of the Night; O Magdalene, the Opener of Ways. Awaken us to greater life!"

Celebrant leads chanting of Her holy names:

"Jaya Kali Ma! Sa Sekhem Sahu! Lilith, Malkah ha-Shadim! Ashray Miriyam! (Victory to Mother Kali! Sa Sekhem Sahu! Lilith, Queen of the Phantoms! Behold Mary!)"

Chant until you have raised the energy in the room, as determined by the Celebrant. Then the Celebrant motions participants to sit and begin meditating privately on their Dark Goddess image. After five to fifteen minutes (or longer if you chose), the Celebrant asks the group to slowly come back to normal consciousness. Participants stand once more in a circle as the Guardians are dismissed and the circle is closed.

MARY MAGDALENE: "Guardians of the East, we thank you for your presence tonight. Go in peace."

SEKHMET: "Guardians of the South, we thank you for your presence tonight. Go in peace."

LILITH: "Guardians of the West, we thank you for your presence tonight. Go in peace."

KALI: "Guardians of the North, we thank you for your presence tonight. Go in peace."

CELEBRANT: "May the circle be open but unbroken and the peace of the Dark One go in our hearts. There is a blessing on those who serve."

The group then shares simple refreshments and their meditative experiences, if desired.

You have now completed the entire *Invoking Mary Magdalene* program. As an initiate on the Magdalene Path, you will turn to these practices again and again. They will comfort and strengthen you in times of crisis, and offer you a devotional connection to the Magdalene whenever you wish to call on her. As you go deeper into these practices, you will experience new realizations and increasingly profound personal relationship to Mary Magdalene. In the final chapter, I offer suggestions for community, fellowship, and continued work with the energies of this most amazing being. ❖

CHAPTER
SEVEN

Continuing on the Magdalene Path

NOW THAT YOU have embarked on the Magdalene Path, what comes next? I recommend that in addition to continuing your studies by reading and regularly engaging in these practices, you find some camaraderie with other Magdalene devotees. Lesa Bellevie, a longtime devotee of the Magdalene, gave an important talk at the 2005 Magdalene feast day celebration in Seattle. In it, she spoke of the essential need to create fellowship within the fledging Magdalene movement (I urge you to read the transcript of her address).[46] You may not know of other Magdalene devotees in your town or metropolis, but they do exist. The Internet boasts many web sites devoted to the Magdalene, including online communities, correspondence courses, and chat groups; I have listed a number of these sites in the Additional Resources section.

Some other ideas for community and continued practice:

- Put up a notice at your local Unitarian, Unity, or other liberal church, the library, food co-op, or other places where progressive folks gather. Ask interested people to meet for a monthly discussion and study group on the Magdalene, using this book or another as a foundation text. Do some of the practices in *Invoking Mary Magdalene* as a group.

- Organize a Magdalene feast day celebration in your town.

- Enroll in a workshop or attend a conference on Mary Magdalene—more and more of these are emerging all the time.

- Embark on a pilgrimage to Magdalene's holy sites, either by yourself, with friends, or with one of the many companies offering tours to her sacred places.

- Set aside one day, a weekend, or longer for a Magdalene retreat. While you can do a retreat at home, it is most efficacious to go to a retreat center. Monasteries and other church retreat centers often arrange for personal retreats at a nominal cost, as well as offering group retreats. Keep in mind other possibilities, like Zen monasteries, yoga ashrams, and national parks, to name a few. Find the Divine web site offers a searchable database of retreat centers in the United States and Canada, and, on the Go Nomad site, you can do a worldwide search for retreat lodging, including farm stays. Both are listed in the Additional Resources section.

- Teach a class at your church, synagogue, or community adult continuing-education center. You do not need to be an expert on a given subject to lead a class. Feel free to use this book to guide your curriculum, if you wish. I recently taught a six-week daytime class on Mary Magdalene at a continuing education school in the Boulder area, and eighteen students, both men and women, enrolled. Since the completion of that class, many of us continue to meet monthly, and even hold a Magdalene feast day celebration in the mountains.

- Finally, please feel free to email me at alexandria@post.harvard.edu. I may not be able to answer each email individually. However, I would enjoy it very much if you let me know about your experiences on the Magdalene Path.

I wish you many blessings on your way and offer you this traditional Jewish prayer as we part for now.

PRAYER OF ARCHANGELIC PROTECTION

Hashem, b'shem, elohai yisrael
Miyimini Michael, mismoli Gavriel,
Ulifani Uriel, umi-acherai Raphael
V'al roshi, v'al roshi shekhinat el.
The Name, in the Name, of the Holy One,
Michael is on my right side, Gabriel my left side,
In front of me, Uriel, behind me, Raphael.
And above my head, above my head, is the Shekhinah, the Divine
  Feminine Presence. ❖

LISTEN TO TRACK 5
Prayer of Archangelic
Protection

Chapter One Notes

1   Martha Shultz, "Working on the Inner Side: The GNOSIS Interview with Nicholas Whitehead," *GNOSIS Magazine,* Fall 1997, 39.

Chapter Two Notes

2   Harold Moldenke, "Flowers of the Madonna," *Horticulture,* December 1953, posted on the Mary Gardens web site, http://www.mgardens.org/HM-FOTM-HO.html (20 February 2006).

Chapter Three Notes

3   Theogamy can also refer to marriage between two gods.

4   Ann E. Matter, "Medieval Women Mystics and the Song of Songs," Lecture at Pendle Hill, 16 October 2000, http://www.pendlehill.org (20 February 2006).

5   Paul M. Allen, *Vladimir Soloviev: Russian Mystic* (Blauvelt, NY: Steinerbooks, 1978), 334.

6   Margaret Starbird, *The Goddess in the Gospels: Reclaiming the Sacred Feminine* (Santa Fe: Bear & Company Publishing, 1998), 145.

7   Copyright by Siobhán Houston.

8   Willis Barnstone, *The Gnostic Bible: Gnostic Texts of Wisdom from the Ancient and Medieval Worlds* (Boston: Shambhala, 2003), 226.

9   The biblical book "Song of Songs" is also known as the "Song of Solomon." The Scripture quotations contained herein [unless otherwise noted] are from the New Revised Standard Version Bible, copyright 1989 by the Division of Christian Education of the National Council of Churches of Christ in the U.S.A. Used with permission. All rights reserved.

10 Andrew Welburn, *Gnosis, the Mysteries and Christianity* (Edinburgh: Floris Books, 1994), 287.

[11] Marvin Meyer, *The Gospels of Mary: The Secret Tradition of Mary Magdalene, the Companion of Jesus* (New York: HarperSanFrancisco, 2004). 73.

[12] Meyer, 20.

[13] Jean Leloup. *The Gospel of Mary Magdalene* (Rochester, Vt: Inner Traditions, 2002), 31.

[14] Tau Malachi, *The Gnostic Gospel of St. Thomas* (St. Paul, MN: Llewellyn, 2004), 189.

[15] Leloup, 31.

[16] Barnstone, 354.

[17] Copyright by Soror Lucia.

[18] Frederick E. Warren, trans. *The Sarum Missal in English.* 2 vol. (Alcum Club Collections XI. London: Mowbray, 1913), II: 417, as quoted in Frank J. Hendersen, "The Disappearance of the Feast Day of Mary Magdalene from the Anglican Liturgy, 2004, http://www.compusmart.ab.ca/fhenders/pdf/Disappearance_Feast_MaryMagdalene.pdf (20 February 2006).

[19] Copyright by Lotus Moonwise (Amy Topham), http://www.moonwisewellness.com.

Chapter Four Notes

[20] Kathy Jones, *The Goddess in Glastonbury.* 1990, http://www.kathyjones.co.uk/goddess_in_glastonbury.html (20 February 2006).

[21] James Twynan, "The Magdalene Experiment," 2003, http://www.emissaryoflight.com (20 February 2006).

[22] Copyright by the Esoteric Mystery School and the Order of Mary Magdalene. Full text at http://www.northernway.org.

[23] Susan Haskins, *Mary Magdalene: Myth and Metaphor,* (New York: Riverhead Books, 1993), 123-125.

Chapter Five Notes

[24] Karen L. King. *The Gospel of Mary of Magdala: Jesus and the First Woman Apostle* (Santa Rosa, Ca: Polebridge Press, 2003), 15.

[25] Meyer, 66.

[26] Ibid., 69.

[27] Ibid., 49.

[28] David Fideler, *Jesus Christ, Sun of God: Ancient Cosmology and Early Christian Symbolism* (Wheaton, Il: Quest Books, 1993), 10.

[29] Caitlin Matthews, *Sophia: Goddess of Wisdom, Bride of God* (Wheaton, IL: Quest Books, 2001), 164.

[30] Copyright by Soror Lucia. Full text with footnotes at http://www.magdalene.org.

[31] Copyright by Ecclesia Gnostica, http://www.gnosis.org.

[32] Omraam Mikhaël Aïvanhov, *A New Earth: Methods, Exercises, Formulas, and Prayers* (Fréjus Cedex, France: Editions Prosveta, 1992), 159.

Chapter Six Notes

[33] Demetra George, *Mysteries of the Dark Moon: The Healing Power of the Dark Goddess* (New York: HarperSanFrancisco, 1992), 34, 50.

[34] Elaine Pagels, *The Gnostic Gospels* (New York: Vintage Books, 1981), 72-73.

[35] Haskins, 81-82.

[36] Ibid., 53.

[37] Ean Begg, *The Cult of the Black Virgin* (London: Arkana, 1996), 58.

[38] Begg, 17-18.

[39] Hilary Hart, *The Unknown She: Eight Faces of an Emerging Consciousness* (Inverness, Ca: The Golden Sufi Center, 2003), 139.

[40] Haskins, 95.

[41] Begg, 99.

[42] Marion Woodman and Elinor Dickson, *Dancing in the Flames: The Dark Goddess in the Transformation of Consciousness* (Boston: Shambhala, 1997), 181.

[43] Copyright by Tau Malachi, http://www.sophian.org/index.html.

[44] Tau Malachi, "Union with the Holy Bride," Sophian Fellowship web site, http://www.sophian.org/Holy%20Bride.htm (20 February 2006).

[45] Copyright by Siobhán Houston.

Chapter Seven Notes

[46] Lesa Bellevie, "On the Need for Fellowship within the Mary Magdalene Movement," transcript of a lecture given on July 23, 2005 in Seattle, WA, http://www.magdalene.org (20 February 2006).

Selected Bibliography

Aïvanhov, Omraam Mikhaël. *A New Earth: Methods, Exercises, Formulas, and Prayers.* Fréjus Cedex, France: Editions Prosveta, 1992.

——. *The Fruits of the Tree of Life: The Cabbalistic Tradition.* Los Angeles: Prosveta, U.S.A., 1991.

Barnstone, Willis. *The Gnostic Bible: Gnostic Texts of Mystical Wisdom from the Ancient and Medieval Worlds.* Boston: Shambhala, 2003.

Begg, Ean. *The Cult of the Black Virgin.* London: Arkana, 1996.

Bellevie, Lesa. *The Complete Idiot's Guide to Mary Magdalene.* New York: Alpha Books, 2005.

Culea, Patti Medaris. *Creative Cloth Doll Making: New Approaches for Using Fibers, Beads, Dyes, and Other Exciting Techniques.* Gloucester, MA: Rockport Publishers, 2003.

Faivre, Antoine, and Jacob Needleman, ed. *Modern Esoteric Spirituality.* New York: SCM Press, 1992.

Fideler, David. *Jesus Christ, Sun of God: Ancient Cosmology and Early Christian Symbolism.* Wheaton, IL: Quest Books, 1993.

Galland, China. *Longing for Darkness: Tara and the Black Madonna.* New York: Penguin, 1990.

George, Demetra. *Mysteries of the Dark Moon: The Healing Power of the Dark Goddess.* New York: HarperSanFrancisco, 1992.

Greer, Mary. *Tarot for Your Self: A Workbook for Personal Transformation.* Franklin Lake, NJ: New Page Books, 2002.

Hart, Hilary. *The Unknown She: Eight Faces of an Emerging Consciousness.* Inverness, CA: The Golden Sufi Center, 2003.

Haskins, Susan. *Mary Magdalene: Myth and Metaphor.* New York: Riverhead Books, 1993.

Hoeller, Stephan A. *Gnosticism: A New Light on an Ancient Tradition of Inner Knowing.* Wheaton, IL: Quest Books, 2002.

Jansen, Katherine Ludwig. *The Making of the Magdalen: Preaching and Popular Devotion in the Later Middle Ages.* Princeton: Princeton University Press, 2000.

Jones, Kathy. *The Goddess in Glastonbury.* (1990). Published online www.kathyjones.co.uk/goddess_in_glastonbury.html (20 February 2006).

Kelly, Liz. *The Rosary: A Path into Prayer.* Chicago: Loyola Press, 2004.

Kenyon, Tom and Judi Sion. *The Magdalen Manuscript: The Alchemies of Horus and the Sex Magic of Isis.* Orcas, WA: ORB Communications, 2002.

Kinstler, Clystra. *The Moon Beneath Her Feet.* New York: HarperSanFrancisco, 1991.

King, Karen L. *The Gospel of Mary of Magdala: Jesus and the First Woman Apostle.* Santa Rosa, CA: Polebridge Press, 2003.

Leloup, Jean-Yves. *The Gospel of Mary Magdalene.* Rochester, VT: Inner Traditions, 2002.

Lundy, Ronni. *Crafts for the Spirit: 30 Beautiful Projects to Enhance Your Personal Journey.* Asheville, NC: Lark Books, 2003.

Matthews, Caitlin. *Sophia: Goddess of Wisdom, Bride of God.* Wheaton, IL: Quest Books, 2001.

Malachi, Tau. *Living Gnosis: A Practical Guide to Gnostic Christianity.* St. Paul: Llewellyn Publications, 2005.

Manning, Tara Jon. *Mindful Knitting: Inviting Contemplative Practice to the Craft.* North Clarendon, VT: Tuttle Publishing, 2004.

McCann, Jean. *Altars and Icons: Sacred Spaces in Everyday Life.* San Francisco: Chronicle Books, 1998.

Meyer, Marvin. *The Gospels of Mary: The Secret Tradition of Mary Magdalene, the Companion of Jesus.* New York: HarperSanFrancisco, 2004.

Pagels, Elaine. *The Gnostic Gospels.* New York: Vintage Books, 1981.

Patai, Raphael. *The Hebrew Goddess.* 3rd ed. Detroit: Wayne State University Press, 1990.

Robinson, James, ed. *The Nag Hammadi Library.* 3rd ed. New York: HarperSanFrancisco, 1990.

Roland, Victor Gold, et al., ed. *The New Testament and Psalms: An Inclusive Version.* New York: Oxford University Press, 1995.

Schaberg, Jane. *Resurrection Of Mary Magdalene: Legends, Apocrypha, and the Christian Testament.* New York: Continuum International Publishing Group, 2002.

Smoley, Richard. *Inner Christianity: A Guide to the Esoteric Tradition.* Boston: Shambhala, 2002.

Starbird, Margaret. *The Feminine Face of Christianity.* Wheaton, IL: Quest Books, 2003.

——. *The Goddess in the Gospels: Reclaiming the Sacred Feminine.* Santa Fe: Bear & Company Publishing, 1998.

——. *Magdalene's Lost Legacy: Symbolic Numbers and the Sacred Union in Christianity.* Santa Fe: Bear & Company Publishing, 2003.

——. *The Woman with the Alabaster Jar: Mary Magdalen and the Holy Grail.* Santa Fe: Bear & Company Publishing, 1993.

Wiley, Eleanor, and Maggie Oman Shannon. *A String and a Prayer: Making and Using Prayer Beads.* York Beach, ME: Red Wheel/Weiser, 2002.

Woodman, Marion, and Elinor Dickson. *Dancing in the Flames: The Dark Goddess in the Transformation of Consciousness.* Boston: Shambhala, 1997.

Web Sites and Organizations

All Seasons Chalice/The Star House in Boulder (workshops, rituals, Magdalene DVD): www.thestarhouse.org

Ani Williams (original Magdalene music, tours, workshops): www.aniwilliams.com

Avalon Mystery School Correspondence Course: www.avalonmysteryschool.net

Celtic Spirit (Mara Freeman): www.celticspirit.org

Dancing Spirit Doll Patterns and Kits: www.softexpressions.com/software/beadcharm/EVDolls.php

The Dharma Shop: www.dharmashop.com

The Dollmaker's Journey: www.dollmakersjourney.com

Ecclesia Gnostica Mysteriorum (and the Holy Order of Mary Magdalene):
3437 Alma, #23
Palo Alto CA 94306
(650) 494-7412
www.gnosticsanctuary.org

The Esoteric Mystery School: www.northernway.org

Find the Divine Retreat Database: www.findthedivine.com/places.html

Future Church: www.futurechurch.org

The Gnostic Apostolic Church of Sophia (online community and mentoring program): www.sophian.org

The Gnostic Society and the Ecclesia Gnostica (Dr. Stephan A. Hoeller):
3363 Glendale Avenue
Los Angeles CA 90039
(323) 467-2685
www.gnosis.org

Go Nomad Alternative Travel: www.gonomad.com

Isolde Hathaway, Doll Artist (Boulder, CO): stewart345@wcox.com

James Twynan and the Beloved Community (the Mary Magdalene experiment): www.emissaryoflight.com

Lotus Moonwise (Amy Topham): lotus@moonwisewellness.com

Magdalene.org (Lesa Bellevie's site): www.magdalene.org

The Magdalene Circle: www.magdalene-circle.org

Margaret Starbird: www.margaretstarbird.net

Mary Gardens: www.mgardens.org

The Order of Mary Magdalene: www.northernway.org/school/omm.html

Our Lady of Guadalupe Site: www.sancta.org/rosary/how.html

Robin Atkins, Bead Artist (spirit doll workshops): www.robinatkins.com

Sacred Source (deities and devotional items): www.sacredsource.com

Shawl Ministry Home Page: www.shawlministry.com

Sophian Fellowship Online Community (Tau Malachi): www.sophian.org/index.html

Tom Kenyon (books, meditation CDs, workshops): www.tomkenyon.com

About the Author

SIOBHÁN HOUSTON is a graduate of Harvard Divinity School and a doctoral candidate in religious studies at the University of Exeter (UK). She is a longtime student of the Western mysteries and has written widely on contemporary religious issues for several national magazines, including *GNOSIS: A Journal of the Western Inner Traditions, Parabola,* and *Intuition Magazine,* among others. Siobhán Houston lives in Boulder, Colorado where she teaches at Naropa University. To learn more about her writings, classes, lectures, and workshops, visit www.siobhanhouston.com.

SOUNDS TRUE was founded with a clear vision: to disseminate spiritual wisdom. Located in Boulder, Colorado, Sounds True publishes teaching programs that are designed to educate, uplift, and inspire. With more than 550 titles available, we work with many of the leading spiritual teachers, thinkers, healers, and visionary artists of our time.

For a free catalog please contact Sounds True via the World Wide Web at www.soundstrue.com, call us toll free at 800-333-9185, or write:

The Sounds True Catalog
PO Box 8010
Boulder CO 80306